**FLOYD CLYMER'S MOTORCYCLIST'S LIBRARY**

# The Book of the
# SUZUKI

## John Thorpe

### ANNOUNCEMENT

By special arrangement with the original publishers of this book, Sir Isaac Pitman & Son, Ltd., of London, England, we have secured the exclusive publishing rights for this book, as well as all others in THE MOTORCYCLIST'S LIBRARY.

Included in THE MOTORCYCLIST'S LIBRARY are complete instruction manuals covering the care and operation of respective motorcycles and engines; valuable data on speed tuning, and thrilling accounts of motorcycle race events. See listing of available titles elsewhere in this edition.

We consider it a privilege to be able to offer so many fine titles to our customers.

### FLOYD CLYMER
Publisher of Books Pertaining to Automobiles and Motorcycles

2125 W. PICO ST.    LOS ANGELES 6, CALIF.

## INTRODUCTION

Welcome to the world of digital publishing ~ the book you now hold in your hand, while unchanged from the original edition, was printed using the latest state of the art digital technology. The advent of print-on-demand has forever changed the publishing process, never has information been so accessible and it is our hope that this book serves your informational needs for years to come. If this is your first exposure to digital publishing, we hope that you are pleased with the results. Many more titles of interest to the classic automobile and motorcycle enthusiast, collector and restorer are available via our website at www.VelocePress.com. We hope that you find this title as interesting as we do.

## NOTE FROM THE PUBLISHER

The information presented is true and complete to the best of our knowledge. All recommendations are made without any guarantees on the part of the author or the publisher, who also disclaim all liability incurred with the use of this information.

## TRADEMARKS

We recognize that some words, model names and designations, for example, mentioned herein are the property of the trademark holder. We use them for identification purposes only. This is not an official publication.

## INFORMATION ON THE USE OF THIS PUBLICATION

This manual is an invaluable resource for the classic motorcycle enthusiast and a "must have" for owners interested in performing their own maintenance. However, in today's information age we are constantly subject to changes in common practice, new technology, availability of improved materials and increased awareness of chemical toxicity. As such, it is advised that the user consult with an experienced professional prior to undertaking any procedure described herein. While every care has been taken to ensure correctness of information, it is obviously not possible to guarantee complete freedom from errors or omissions or to accept liability arising from such errors or omissions. Therefore, any individual that uses the information contained within, or elects to perform or participate in do-it-yourself repairs or modifications acknowledges that there is a risk factor involved and that the publisher or its associates cannot be held responsible for personal injury or property damage resulting from the use of the information or the outcome of such procedures.

## WARNING!

One final word of advice, this publication is intended to be used as a reference guide, and when in doubt the reader should consult with a qualified technician.

# Preface

So far as motor-cycling and motoring are concerned, the 'sixties will be remembered as the decade which saw Japan emerge as a formidable competitor for world markets. Even at the start of the decade Japanese machines were almost unknown in Europe, yet within five years or so if one wanted the best in the way of motor-cycles one was almost certainly forced to consider two or three Japanese marques in any short list of half a dozen machines.

One of those marques would definitely be Suzuki. In slightly more than three years since the first of these smart horseshoe-headlamp two-strokes reached the British market over 30,000 of them were on our roads—pretty good going, by any yardstick. From obscurity to top-selling two-stroke in three years—even with the backing of a lively indigenous marketing organization—is a very considerable achievement.

But there is nothing of the "fluke" about it. The Suzuki appeals to motor-cyclists because it is made like a precision watch yet has the toughness of a ship's chronometer. It is this almost unique blend of delicacy and indestructability—of simplicity and sophistication—which accounts for its success.

And, of course, there is the safety aspect. These lightweights *really* handle. They have the sort of road-holding and braking which rightly belongs to the racing circuit—and when one looks at their manufacturer's enviable record of world championships and (particularly important to a British rider) T.T. wins one can see why. They were born on the circuits. . . .

In this book I have dealt with all the most popular models—the 50 c.c. M 12, M 15 and M 15 D motor-cycles; the charming little M 30 Suzy scooterette ("mokick," if you prefer Suzuki's own description!); and the peppy 80 c.c. K 10 and K 11 machines. I have not, however, included working instructions on the S 30 125 c.c. motor-cycle nor the T 10 250 c.c. twin. Neither have I dealt with the 1966 newcomers—the 125 c.c. B 100 P and the T 20 Super Six twin. A separate book on these larger models at some time in the future is, however, a project I shall keep in mind. Meantime, the owners of these models in the Suzuki range will find that all but the specialized chapters in this book will help them understand and maintain their machines when used in conjunction with the ordinary

## PREFACE

rider's handbook. Detailed instructions for work on the gearbox are not given since it is unlikely that the average private owner will ever need to carry out such operations. However, working instructions sufficient to permit replacement of shafts and bearings are included.

I may add that in the preparation of this book I have been admirably aided by Suzuki (Gt. Britain) Ltd., Golden Hillock Road, Birmingham 11. They have provided me with manuals and permission to use their illustrations; and Alan Kimber even raided his own library to produce one or two of the rarer sources of information. That's service—Suzuki service!

Surrenden Park　　　　　　　　　　　　　　　　　　　　JOHN THORPE
Brighton
Sussex

# Contents

| | | |
|---|---|---|
| 1 | How the Suzuki Works | 1 |
| 2 | The Tools You Need | 16 |
| 3 | Methodical Maintenance | 19 |
| 4 | Overhauling Carburettors | 23 |
| 5 | Electrical Overhauls | 32 |
| 6 | Renovating the 50 c.c. Motor-cycle Engines | 41 |
| 7 | Overhauling the Suzy Engine | 52 |
| 8 | Overhauling the 80 c.c. Engine | 57 |
| 9 | The Cycle Parts | 63 |
| 10 | Trouble Tracing | 73 |
| | *Appendix:* Facts and Figures | 84 |
| | *Index* | 86 |

# 1 How the Suzuki works

DISMANTLE your Suzuki and you will be impressed by the attention to detail which has gone into its design and construction. Somebody obviously sat and pondered at his drawing-board, anxious to produce a machine which would be well-fitted for its purpose. And when the concept was right, somebody else obviously put a great deal of time and care into making sure that it was mechanically correct too. After that, modern

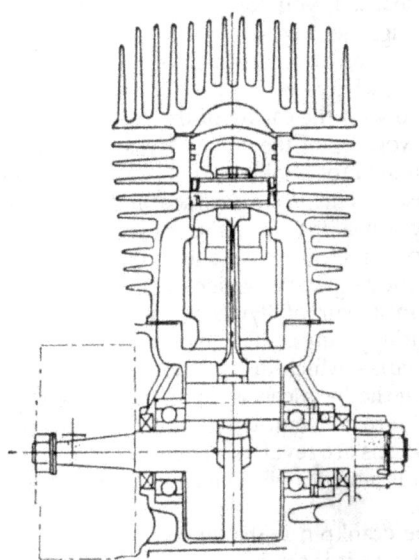

FIG. 1. A TYPICAL SUZUKI TWO-STROKE ENGINE

This is the 80 c.c. K 10 power unit in cross section. It is typical of the engines produced by Suzuki, and its sturdy construction is immediately apparent.

engineering took over and ensured that the machine which came off the assembly line was the machine that the designers had specified. The result? A small two-stroke with a big performance; a machine which, given the due care any fine piece of mechanism demands, will give long life and reliable service (see Fig. 1).

This is where the Suzuki owner has a part to play. No machine can continue to operate at maximum efficiency if it is neglected. But, at the other extreme, it won't do so if it is subjected to constant tinkering. The right balance has to be struck—and it is the purpose of this book to help you attain it.

Before you can hope to maintain a machine properly, however, you *must* know how it works and understand why the various parts are made the way they are and what their purpose is. Without such knowledge, constructive maintenance is made more difficult and fault tracing is impossible.

Suzuki make only two-stroke engines. Now a "stroke" is one complete part of a working cycle—rather like a bar of music or a sentence in writing. A two-stroke engine, then, has two strokes to each complete cycle of operation. The other main type of engine—the four-stroke—has four strokes to a working cycle. Oddly enough, it helps to know the four-stroke cycle first. That learned, you can understand the two-stroke cycle more clearly. First, though, let's consider how an engine is constructed.

Basically, you can break it down into moving and non-moving parts. Start at the bottom, where you have a light alloy crankcase. On Suzukis, this is incorporated with the casing of the gearbox, but that does not have any effect on the working of the engine. Mounted on the crankcase is the cylinder, heavily finned for cooling. It is closed at one end by a lid known as the cylinder head. This, too, is finned and it is also bored through to provide a location for a sparking plug. Fit all these parts together and, outwardly, you would seem to have an engine. But it wouldn't work— not without the moving parts which fit inside it. Basically, these are nothing more than a pair of flywheels, a connecting rod, and a piston equipped with springy rings. The flywheels are supported on shafts— called the main shafts—which in turn are carried on bearings set into the crankcase. Joining the flywheels is a pin, called the crankpin. Unlike the main shafts, which are concentric with the flywheels, this is offset. When, therefore, the flywheels are revolved the main shafts merely turn round and round, but the crankpin goes off on a circular trip, rather like a space-ship orbiting the earth.

Mounted on the crankpin is the connecting rod. This has one big end and one small end. As it is the big end which is fitted to the crankpin, the bearing at this point is called the big-end bearing. Fairly predictably, the bearing at the other end of the rod is called the small-end bearing. Through the small end a pin is inserted. This pin also passes through the bosses of the piston, and the piston slides up and down inside the cylinder. Around the base of the cylinder holes are cut. These are called ports. There are three types—the induction port, which connects the crankcase to the inlet pipe; the transfer ports, which connect the crankcase with the cylinder; and the exhaust port, which connects the cylinder with the exhaust pipe. These ports are opened and closed by the piston sliding over them, unlike the four-stroke in which there are only induction and exhaust ports which are opened and closed by valves.

Let's consider, now, how the engine works—and to make things clearer let's start with the four-stroke cycle. There are two main reference points to remember. When the piston is right at the top of its travel it is said to be at Top Dead Centre (T.D.C.) and when it is right at the bottom of its travel it is at Bottom Dead Centre (B.D.C.). The cycle starts with the piston at T.D.C. and the inlet port open. As the crankshaft is revolved, the crankpin starts its circular movement and, in doing so, pulls the connecting rod down the cylinder. The rod, in turn, pulls the piston with it. This, obviously, increases the space between the top of the piston (the crown) and the cylinder head. Increasing the space means that the pressure in it is reduced, and consequently air flows in from outside, through the inlet pipe, to equalize the pressure. In passing through, it is mixed with petrol to form a combustible mixture. It continues to be induced all the time the piston is moving down the cylinder, and this first stroke is therefore called the Induction Stroke.

At B.D.C., the crankpin has moved as far downwards as it can and, therefore, must now start to move upwards again. At this point, the induction port is shut off by a valve, and as the piston rises in the cylinder the mixture trapped inside the engine is compressed into, perhaps, one eighth of its natural volume. This compression is vital to the working of the engine—uncompressed mixture will not burn effectively. Again, fairly predictably, this stroke is known as the Compression Stroke.

When the piston again reaches T.D.C. the mixture is fired by a spark at the points of the sparking plug. Burning rapidly, the petrol vapour expands and presses hard against all the surrounding surfaces. Of these, only one can move—the piston crown. Therefore, the burning gas forces the piston down the cylinder. This time, it is the piston which presses on the connecting rod, and the rod transmits the thrust to the offset crankpin. This turns, spinning the flywheels and main shafts and so driving the machine. Obviously, this is the Power Stroke.

By the time the piston reaches B.D.C. the energy behind the gases in the cylinder is exhausted. As the piston rises again the exhaust port is opened and the piston—operated now by the momentum of the still-spinning flywheels—pushes the burned gas out of the engine and into the exhaust pipe. This is the Exhaust Stroke. At T.D.C. the exhaust port is closed, the inlet port opened, and another cycle of operations starts with a fresh Inlet Stroke.

There you have your four basic strokes—Induction, Compression, Power, Exhaust. Of the four, only one is a power stroke. Since there is one stroke to each half turn of the flywheels, it follows that in a four-stroke engine there is one power stroke in each two revolutions of the crankshaft. The idea behind the two-stroke engine is to get more power strokes—one to each revolution of the shaft—and, at the same time, to obviate the need for valves to open and close the ports and so produce a simpler engine.

The two-stroke is certainly simple. It consists of the crankcase, cylinder, cylinder head, flywheel assembly, connecting rod and piston—and nothing else. No valves and their associated mechanism—their place is taken by the piston-controlled ports.

Let's take our two-stroke, with its piston at T.D.C. We will have to imagine that the cylinder is already charged and that the spark has just occurred. One thing is already happening. The inlet port is open, and petrol/air mixture is flowing through it because—the crankcase being sealed in all other directions—the pressure inside it is lower than the pressure of the atmosphere outside. In the cylinder, the piston is driven down by the expanding gases. As it does so, its bottom edge covers the inlet port, trapping the new mixture in the crankcase. All the time the piston is descending this mixture is compressed more and more.

As the piston nears the end of its journey down the cylinder bore, its upper edge uncovers the exhaust port. Immediately, the gases begin to rush out of it—carried by their own momentum. A split second later, further downward movement of the piston uncovers the transfer ports. Since its underside is compressing the mixture trapped in the crankcase, the piston itself pumps this gas through the transfers and into the cylinder. The transfer ports are so set that the gas streams collide and deflect upwards, taking the fresh gas clear of the still-open exhaust port.

As the piston moves upwards, it closes first the transfers and then the exhaust port. Next, it compresses the fresh charge in the cylinder—already partly compressed before being transferred from the crankcase. As the piston nears T.D.C. its bottom edge again uncovers the inlet port, and another charge flows through the inlet pipe and enters the crankcase. At T.D.C. another spark ignites the mixture in the combustion chamber above the piston, and the cycle recommences.

Obviously, this is not as clear-cut a process as in the four-stroke. Two things are always happening at once. Thus, each downward movement of the piston is a Power Stroke and each upward movement a Compression Stroke. There is no Induction Stroke as such—it is replaced by an induction period around T.D.C. There is no Exhaust Stroke as such. That is replaced by an exhaust period shortly before B.D.C. And in addition, there is a transfer period around B.D.C. It is perhaps easiest to remember the cycle of operations by referring to what is happening at top and bottom—in the cylinder and in the crankcase, respectively. Then, by slightly over-simplifying matters, you get the following result—Top, Compression; Bottom, Induction. Top, Power; Bottom, Compression (*see* Fig. 2).

An engine such as the one just described would work—given the means of mixing the petrol and air and igniting the mixture. But it would not work for long. All that burning and movement mean heat, and if metal-to-contact were maintained throughout the unit the surfaces would soon become so hot that they would melt and fuse into each other. In other words, they would seize. What prevents them from doing so is lubrication—by means of oil. Now, in four-stroke engines this has to be circulated by means of a pump—another complication with which the simpler two-stroke can dispense. In the two-stroke, advantage is taken of the fact that, initially, the mixture goes into the crankcase. So, a certain quantity of oil is mixed with the petrol in the fuel tank, and, therefore, some oil enters the crankcase with the petrol/air mixture. Under the combined effects of compression and centrifugal action by the flywheels some of this oil is condensed out to form an oil film all over the working parts. It therefore separates the metal components, interposing itself as a thin but strong barrier over which the parts slide easily. It thus reduces friction and, in doing so, lessens the amount of heat generated. In addition, it

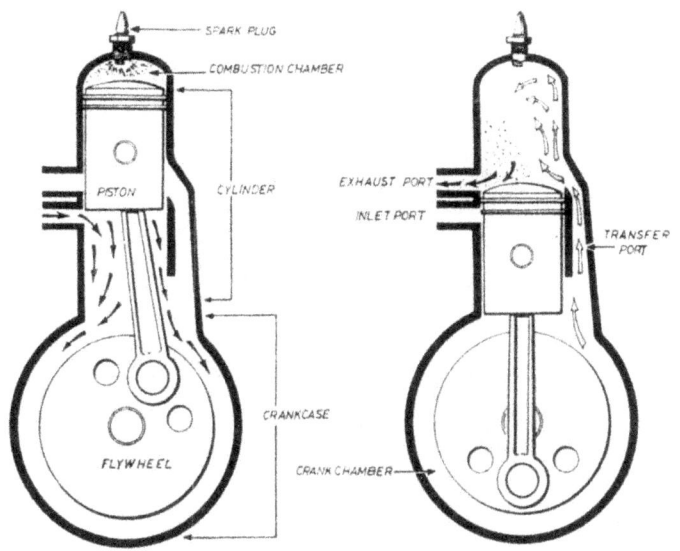

FIG. 2. THE TWO-STROKE CYCLE

The gas flow through a two-stroke engine, showing how the normal four working strokes are "telescoped" to provide a power stroke each time the piston comes to Top Dead Centre

absorbs some of the remaining heat from the internal components and distributes it to the static parts, whence it is dissipated by radiation into the air.

Obviously, the oil has a big job to do. That's what makes it so important to adhere rigidly to the manufacturer's recommended oil quantity in the fuel and also to use the correct grade. Oils have different characteristics, and exhaustive tests are carried out to ensure that the right oil is matched to the right engine. This is especially important in the case of a two-stroke, in which the bearings need a greater degree of protection from corrosion and from the "washing" effect of the petrol in the mixture.

## CARBURATION

So far, we have not considered two vital parts of the engine. One of these is the carburettor—a compact precision instrument which does an exacting job (*see* Figs. 3, 4 and 5). Its purpose is to meter petrol so that at all times the "ideal" ratio of 14 parts of air to one of petrol is maintained. This may not appear to be much of a chore, at least at first sight. But there's a snag—that ratio is in terms of weight, whereas the engine—and, therefore, the carburettor—has to work by volume. Now air is much lighter

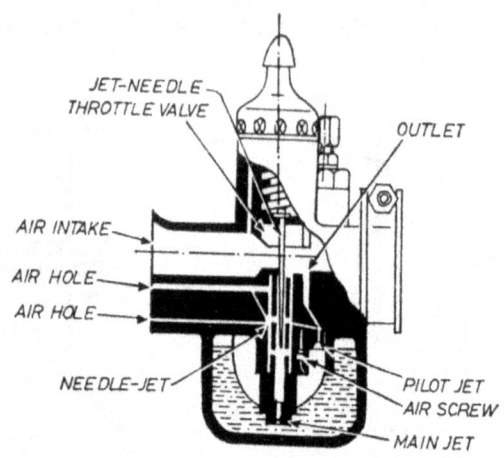

Fig. 3. How a Carburettor is Set Out

The longitudinal position of all the main components of the Amal carburettor is shown here.

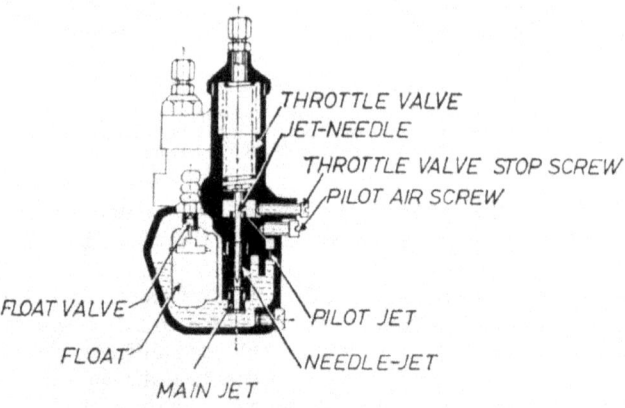

Fig. 4. A Carburettor in End Section

This Amal has been "cut" across its centre line to show the lateral disposition of the components.

than petrol, and on a basis of volume every 100 c.c. of mixture must contain just 0·01 c.c. of petrol which must be mixed with 99·99 c.c. of air! To obtain this calls for some delicating metering.

The basic parts of a carburettor (*see* Fig. 7) are a petrol reservoir, called

## HOW THE SUZUKI WORKS

a float chamber; a venturi (or choke) through which air is drawn; jets, which meter petrol into the air stream; and a throttle, which controls the

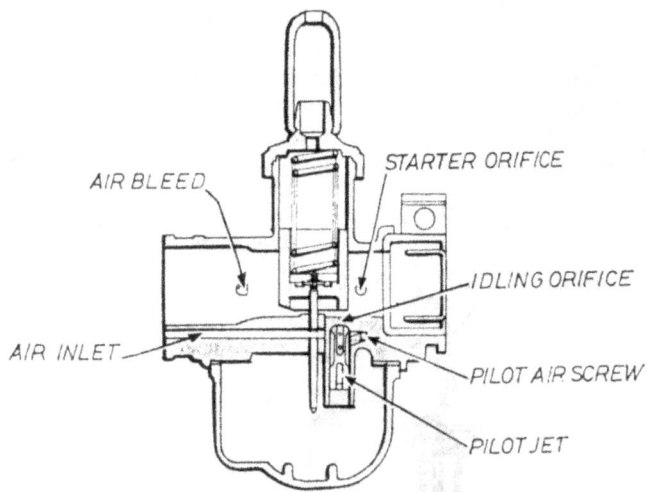

FIG. 5. THE UPPER PART OF THE CARBURETTOR
The layout of the main carburettor components follows this general pattern.

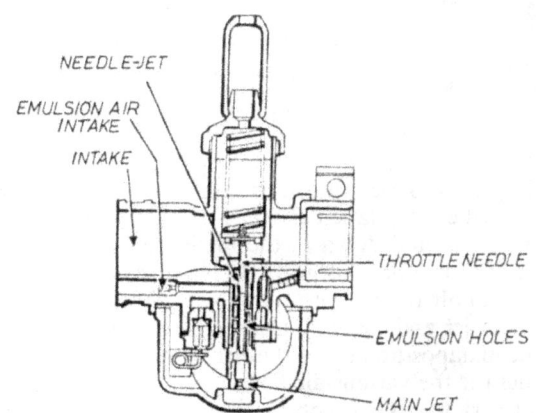

FIG. 6. THE LOWER HALF OF THE CARBURETTOR
The jets and metering channels are largely contained in the lower half of the instrument and are semi-immersed in the float chamber.

amount of mixture admitted to the engine—which, obviously, only receives a full charge when operating at full throttle.

The method of working is that petrol is fed by gravity from the fuel tank into the float chamber, which is much like a miniature domestic cistern. It contains a float which rises with the level of the petrol in the chamber, and the float carries a needle. When the fuel level reaches a predetermined point, the float holds the needle hard inside a special seating in the fuel inlet, and thus cuts off the flow until the level falls through petrol being used up. As the level falls, so does the float, withdrawing the needle from its seating and admitting sufficient fuel to restore the level before the flow is again cut off.

A passageway connects the float chamber with a jet well, in which is located the main jet—basically, a screw through which a tiny metering

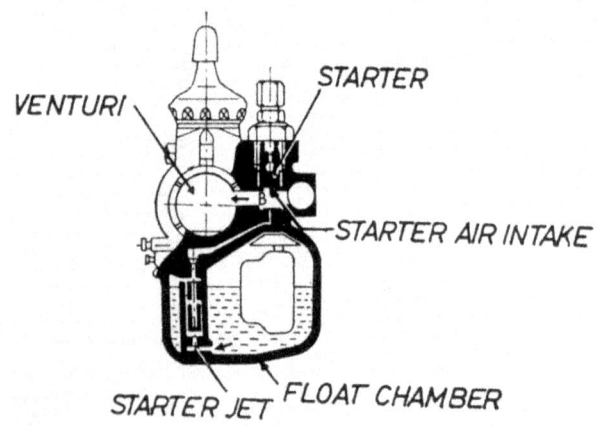

FIG. 7. THE AMAL STARTER SYSTEM

For starting, a rich mixture is necessary. This is supplied by the starting system, which is shown in black. The mixture is delivered through passage "*B*."

hole has been bored. This jet is screwed into the needle-jet tube, whose opposite end opens into the venturi. It is tapered internally, and operating inside it is a needle (also tapered) which is clipped to the throttle slide. This slide moves up and down in the mixing chamber according to the movement of the throttle twistgrip. It has a cut-away which allows a certain amount of air to pass into the mixing chamber, and the combination of the main jet and the variable aperture of the needle-jet resulting from different juxtapositioning of the needle and the tube gives the right amount of fuel for the various air flows. For example, when the throttle is fully open the slide offers no obstruction in the venturi, since it is lifted completely clear. The throttle needle, too, is clear of the tapered needle-jet and thus full air flow is combined with full fuel flow through the main jet to provide the engine with the greatest possible amount of mixture. At tick-over, on the other hand, the needle cuts off the fuel supply completely and only a little air gets past the slide, which is lowered almost to the floor of the venturi. This small quantity of air is mixed with a minute spray of petrol fed direct into the mixing chamber through a very fine metering device called the pilot jet.

## HOW THE SUZUKI WORKS

For starting, a rich mixture—one containing a greater quantity of petrol—is required (*see* Figs. 7 and 8). This is obtained by artificially restricting the air flow with a strangler—a supplementary slide.

So that the jets will not be blocked by dirt in the petrol, all fuel entering the carburettor is filtered. So, too, is the air—though here the main purpose is to protect the engine. Air contains dust, and dust in its turn contains myriad specks of very hard material. This could cause heavy wear in the two-stroke's internals; hence, they are filtered out before they have a chance to do any harm. As the air filter traps these particles, it

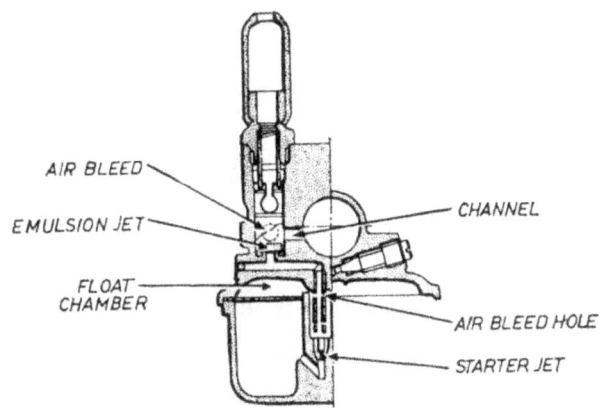

FIG. 8. THE SLOW-RUNNING CIRCUIT
This is the detail layout of the Amal starter device, which provides a rich mixture for a cold engine.

gradually becomes blocked, and if air cleaner maintenance is neglected it can restrict the air flow, richen the mixture, and waste petrol as well as reducing power.

### THE IGNITION SYSTEM

Even highly experienced riders often have only a hazy idea how the electrical system works. It is divided into two parts—lighting and ignition (*see* Fig. 9)—and both tend to be taken for granted until they fail to work, being given little thought or maintenance. When, understandably, they object to such neglect the assumption is made that electricity is not to be trusted. That, to say the least, is grossly unfair to a very efficient power station in miniature—which is what your Suzuki's electrical system in fact is.

All electrical practice is founded upon circuits and upon the fact that an electrical current will invariably take the shortest path to earth. It should be emphasized, though, that "earth" here does not mean the ground. So far as the Suzuki's electrical system is concerned "earth" is the machine itself—a little world all of its own, insulated from the real earth by its rubber tyres.

A circuit is just what its name implies. In this, electricity is rather like a model train. If all the points are properly set and the current is switched on the train will go round and round. If the points are not properly set it will either end up standing still or will go off on the wrong path. And if there is no current it won't work at all.

As with the model, so with electricity. Providing there is a complete circuit the current will flow. If the circuit is broken it won't—save in the

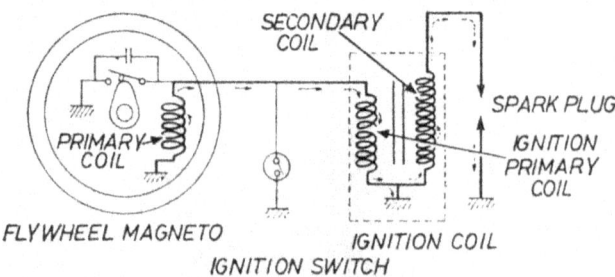

FIG. 9. THE COMPLETE IGNITION SYSTEM

In this diagrammatic view, the ignition system is shown as a whole, and the current flow in the low- and high-tension circuits is indicated by arrows.

case of a small gap in the high-tension system at the sparking plug points, over which it jumps because of its own sheer momentum.

Electricity is measured in volts and amperes. The volt is a measure of force; the ampere indicates the quantity of electricity which is flowing. Multiply the two together and you get a composite picture called a watt. For example, to light a 24-watt bulb in a 6-volt system requires the flow of $24 \div 6 = 4$ amperes. The resistance to current flow presented by the wires and terminals is measured in ohms—a resistance of one ohm being one which calls for one volt pressure to be applied so that one ampere may flow. All the electrical leads have some resistance, but it is worth remembering that the smaller the diameter of the lead the higher the resistance is, and the larger the diameter the less it is.

You will also meet the terms "positive" and "negative." Apart from remembering that they exist, there is nothing to do but connect positive and negative terminals properly when working on the machine. Finally, one must accept one basic fact—that when a coil is placed in a magnetic field electricity is produced. That is how your Suzuki's generator works. There are two types—the flywheel magneto (*see* Figs. 10 and 11) and the a.c. generator. The former produces a current which flows in one direction only; the latter generates a current which constantly reverses its flow.

In the flywheel magneto, permanent magnets are mounted inside the rim of the external flywheel and a stator plate holding coils is bolted to the engine. A form of mechanical switch called a "contact-breaker" is also carried on the stator and operated by a cam formed on the flywheel boss

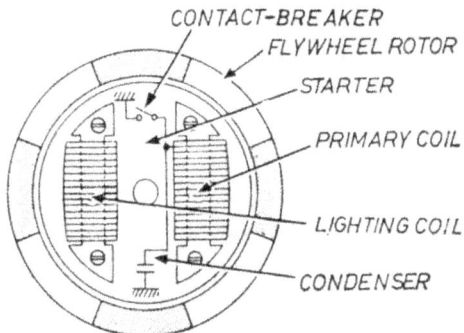

FIG. 10. THE FLYWHEEL MAGNETO
A diagrammatic drawing, showing the layout of a typical Suzuki flywheel magneto.

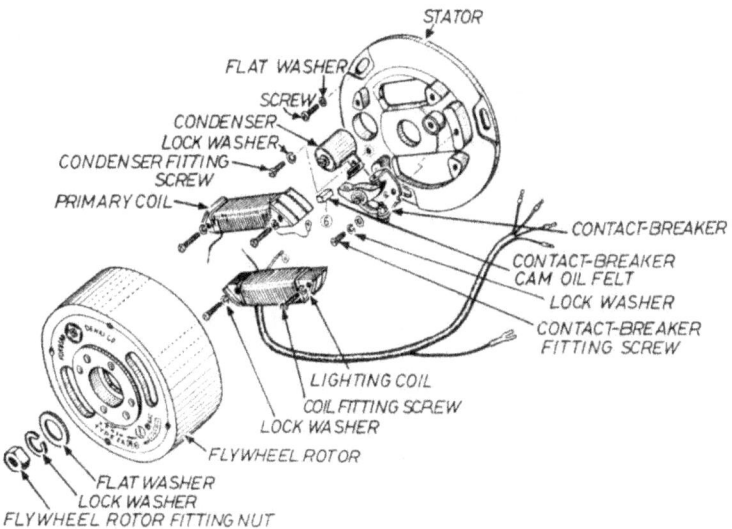

FIG. 11. THE FLYWHEEL MAGNETO "EXPLODED"
This is the type of magneto fitted to the M 30 Suzy.

(see Figs. 12 and 13). This is linked to an outside coil known as the ignition coil. From this, a heavily-insulated lead goes to the sparking plug in the cylinder head. The sparking plug itself consists of a central electrode to which the high-tension lead connects, and a body screwed into the cylinder head and carrying a side electrode. The centre electrode is insulated from the body, and a gap is left between the two electrodes (*see* Fig. 14).

When the flywheel is revolved the magnets set up a magnetic field and low-tension electricity (electricity at low pressure) is generated in the coils.

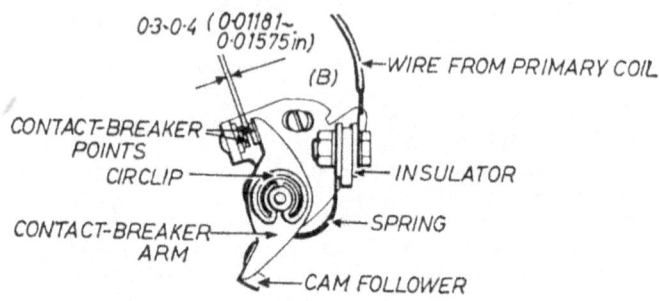

Fig. 12. The Contact-Breaker

This type of contact-breaker is common to all the Suzukis. The setting between the points is critical. If it is wrong it can seriously affect the ignition timing. It is shown in millimetres and inches.

At a predetermined point, however, this current is interrupted by the contact-breaker points being forced apart by the cam. Normally, of course, this sudden breaking of the circuit would mean that no current would flow. But the ignition coil is of special construction. It is really

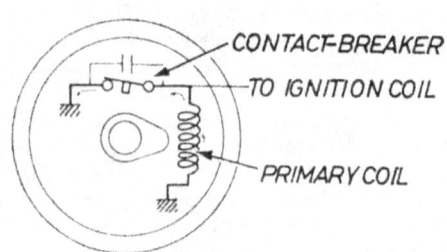

Fig. 13. The Contact-Breaker

A diagrammatic illustration of the contact-breaker and its electrical connexions, showing how it is fed from the primary coil on the L.T. side.

two coils in one—a low-tension primary winding and, inside that, a high-tension secondary winding. The breakdown of the low-tension circuit caused by the points opening in fact causes a high-tension current to be generated in the secondary windings. This is at really high pressure—over 14,000 volts. It streaks down the H.T. lead and jumps the gap between the sparking plug points as a fat blue spark. And that spark ignites the mixture in the cylinder. In your Suzuki engine this happens about 5,000 times every minute. Incidentally, to prevent the low-tension current doing at the contact-breaker points just what the high-tension current does at the spark plug gap a small electrical "shock absorber" called a condenser is added to the circuit.

The generator works in much the same way, but with a difference. It

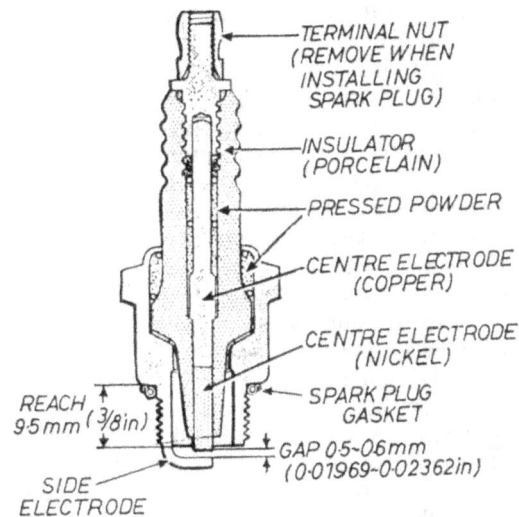

Fig. 14. A Sparking Plug in Cross Section

Two-stroke engines are very sensitive to their plugs, and it is essential that the plug is kept in good condition. Clean it regularly and set the gap accurately.

is a more efficient instrument at low speeds but it has to have its current rectified for battery charging, and this demands the incorporation of a selenium rectifier which is simply an electrical non-return valve.

### THE TRANSMISSION

At low speeds—and low, in this context, means anything under 1,000 r.p.m.—internal combustion engines develop relatively little torque (turning power) compared with their performance higher up the rev. range. Basically, there is a quite narrow range of engine speeds at which the greater power is developed, and the engine should run in that range wherever possible. Since road conditions vary from a traffic crawl to fast work on open roads, and from dropping downhill on next to no throttle to climbing a 1 in 4 hill on full throttle the engine rev. range alone is obviously not enough to ensure this. The answer is provided by the gearbox, which gives the rider a choice of power applications.

Basically, the gearbox consists of an input and an output shaft, each carrying a series of gears. Those on the input shaft mesh with those on the output shaft and each gives a different reduction between the speed of the shafts. Only one pair can be locked at a time.

The drive comes, in the first place, from the crankshaft, being transmitted through the primary gears. This provides the first speed reduction. The gearbox provides the second. Then the drive passes to the sprockets and chain of the secondary transmission before it reaches the rear wheel. What set out as, say, 4,000 revolutions of the crankshaft every minute is delivered as anything from 1,000 to 200 turns of the rear wheel every minute. This accounts for the term "reduction gearing."

Why reduce the revs. in this way? Because revs. in themselves are useless. Power is what counts. In top gear, with the machine well under way and carried to an extent by its own momentum one would be applying the power of four strokes of the piston to every revolution of the rear wheel, and that would be sufficient. But when climbing that 1 in 4 hill in bottom gear, the power of 20 strokes of the piston would be applied for every revolution of the wheel. The lower the gear the less the speed but the greater the pulling power is a simple way of looking at it.

A vital part of the transmission is the clutch—a series of plain and friction-faced discs held together in a drum by spring pressure. One set of plates is fixed to the clutch drum, but not to its centre hub. The other set is fixed to the centre, but not to the drum. The drum is driven by the primary gearing, while the centre is attached to the gearbox input shaft. There is, therefore, no mechanical connexion between the clutch drum (and, hence, the primary drive) and the gearbox. All the drive has to be transmitted through the clutch plates, which are held together by friction alone. Normally, the springs hold the plates together so closely that the clutch drum, the plates and the centre revolve as one unit. When they do, the drive is transmitted from the engine to the gearbox. When the clutch lever is operated (or at very low engine r.p.m., in the case of an automatic clutch) the spring pressure is relieved and there is then no longer sufficient frictional contact between the plates to keep up the drive. The plates which are fixed to the clutch drum are still driven by it, and continue to revolve with it, but the plates attached to the clutch centre simply stand still. And when that happens, so does the clutch centre itself and, consequently, the gearbox input shaft. No drive at all reaches the gearbox. It stops short at the revolving clutch drum.

As the clutch lever is released on a manual-clutch machine, the effect is to increase the spring pressure again and so bring the plates once more into contact. At first, they transmit only a little drive, since they are slipping on each other. When full spring pressure is applied they are again solid and the clutch is transmitting the full drive power. This is what happens every time the machine is ridden away from rest.

On an automatic clutch machine, speeding up the engine causes balls to be forced outwards along tracks by centrifugal force, and it is these which control the clutch in the same way as the hand on a lever controls it with a manual model. The actual principle of operation is identical in both cases.

## THE CYCLE PARTS

Why doesn't a motor-cycle topple over when it is being ridden along a road? For exactly the same reason that a gyroscope doesn't. Its two revolving wheels in fact act as a pair of gyroscopes and resist attempts to force them off their course.

There are other factors, of course. One is the steering design. Motor-cycle steering is so arranged that the front wheel "trails" relative to the steering head of the frame, and the characteristics of the machine depend to a great extent upon the angle at which the head is raked and the amount of trail the designer has built in. The greater the trail and the rake the greater the self-centring action of the steering becomes and the harder the machine is to turn. Other important considerations are the position of the centre of gravity and its co-relationship with the centre of roll. But all that is the designer's headache, not ours!

Two types of front suspension are used on Suzuki machines—the swinging link front fork and the telescopic fork. The former has the advantage of keeping the wheelbase almost constant at all times. The "tele." allows the wheelbase to vary, but generally gives more accurate steering. In each case, the link or the plunger carrying the wheel spindle can only rise against the resistance of a suspension spring, and its return is slowed down—"damped"—by a hydraulic damper. This is a sealed device rather like an elaborate tyre pump, except that what it is pumping is oil, not air. On the upward stroke the damper piston forces oil from one chamber to another through large orifices, so that there is very little resistance to movement of the spring. On the downward stroke, however, a valve closes these large passages and the oil is forced to return through small ones. This causes a great deal of controlled friction, and the drag prevents the spring from hurling the spindle down quickly and so causing unwanted bouncing. A similar form of damping is also used on the rear suspension.

Just as important as being able to move is being able to stop. Therefore, the machine has brakes—a pair of drums. Each has a carefully formed working surface inside, on to which a pair of friction-faced shoes can be "expanded" by the action of a cam linked to the brake control. As the control is operated, the cam turns and the shoes are forced into contact with the revolving drum. The friction which results absorbs energy which would otherwise be moving the machine, and the result is that it slows and stops. The energy so absorbed is turned into heat and is dissipated through the material of the drum and, through the fins formed on it, into the air.

## 2 The tools you need

IT is virtually impossible to make a bigger mistake, when setting out to maintain or overhaul a motor-cycle, than to attempt to do the job with inadequate tools. To carry out even routine maintenance jobs properly calls for the use of a good-quality tool kit, while major overhauls can quite often require the use of special tools. This is certainly the case with the Suzuki, since stripping demands the use of some tools designed by the manufacturer to do one specific job, and one job only.

Each Suzuki is equipped with a tool kit upon delivery, but this is designed to cope only with roadside emergencies and to carry out the simpler routine jobs. It is not intended for the sterner work of stripping the engine.

The use of special service tools is not dictated by cantankerousness on the part of the manufacturer. Nor does it indicate a desire to make a little on the side by selling such tools at an extra profit. It merely reflects the fact that these motor-cycles are precision-engineered. To obtain the performance and reliability of the Suzuki the specified tolerances are very close; so close, in fact, that only special tools have the slightest hope of freeing the various components concerned. So, where a special tool is specified in the overhaul chapters you *must* use it. Alternatives are suggested wherever this is possible.

Even where the jobs to be tackled do not call for the use of special tools they will still require the use of good tools. Cheap spanners and so forth are a bad investment. They do not wear well, and they are also liable to ruin nuts and bolts. Thus, the first essential is to buy a really good set of chrome-vanadium open-ended spanners in metric sizes. A set of half a dozen spanners will give a range of sizes sufficient for most of the work, and will cost only a couple of pounds.

Next, it is vital to have a set of strong metric box spanners, or, better still, deep socket spanners. Ring spanners are more of a luxury. They are less handy in confined spaces than are open-enders or sockets, although they do give a very good grip. In addition, you will need a set of really good screwdrivers, with insulated handles. One screwdriver with a $\frac{5}{16}$-in. blade; an electrical screwdriver with a long $\frac{1}{8}$-in. blade; and a pair of cross-headed screwdrivers of two sizes—these are the minimum requirements. And don't forget your pliers. They are indispensable for electrical work and for use on the control cables.

### USING THE TOOLS

There is far more to using even the simplest of hand tools than merely placing them in position and tugging hard. Each particular type of spanner has its own characteristics, and each is better suited for one particular type of job.

Open-ended spanners are the great all-rounders of the kit. They can be used in confined spaces and they have the advantage that the jaws are angled, so that reversing the spanner will give fresh purchase on the nut. This is most useful when the nut in question is rather inaccessible, since it can be freed in stages simply by constantly reversing the spanner.

It is, of course, essential that only the right size of spanner should be used. The open-ender applies its pressure on the flats of the nut or bolt-head, and consequently it is made with jaws of just the right width to grip them. If too large a spanner is used, the jaws will press against the angles of the flats instead of the flats themselves. One of two things then happens: either the spanner gouges away the metal of the head, leaving a rounded surface which no spanner on earth could ever again grip, or else the bolt-head slightly springs the jaws of the spanner itself, which is promptly ruined. Or, of course, you can get the worst of both worlds and ruin both bolt and spanner together!

Damage to the jaws can also be caused by applying excessive force when trying to free a bolt which refuses to budge. There is a temptation, under these circumstances, to slip a piece of piping over the free end of the spanner to increase the leverage. This is sometimes permissible provided due care is used, but if you are none too experienced as a mechanic it is inadvisable to try it. You are more likely to spring the spanner's jaws. Use a socket spanner instead, and you will be surprised at the result.

Sockets and box or ring spanners are at a great advantage when it comes to shifting recalcitrant nuts. Both rings and sockets grip on the angles—not the flats—of the bolt and consequently apply pressure at half a dozen points where the open-ended spanner can do so only on two surfaces. A box spanner can apply its force on both angles and flats, provided it fits well (cheap box spanners rarely do) but frequently the weak point here is the tommy-bar used to turn the box, which simply bends under the strain. Another drawback with box spanners is that, owing to the offset between the part of this spanner which holds the nut and the holes through which the tommy-bar passes, the spanner may tend to ride off the hexagon when pressure is applied.

When using a spanner to tighten nuts or bolts it is important to remember that too much force should not be used. Spanners are made long enough to ensure that mere hand pressure applied through its full leverage is sufficient to lock the size of nut or bolt for which the spanner is intended. If excessive force is used, the actual material of the bolt can be weakened sufficiently to cause a fracture. This point, too, should be borne in mind particularly when tightening bolts which are threaded into light alloy. Here, the steel bolt is much harder than the material forming the internal threads, and over-enthusiasm with the spanner can easily strip the threads in the hole. The only real solution, then, is to drill out the hole and re-tap it to take a larger-sized bolt.

Pliers, of course, should never be used as a makeshift spanner, since the jaws can never be parallel and the serrated pipe grip is almost perilously liable to slip. A rounded hexagon is the inevitable result if it does.

Adjustable spanners should never be allowed near the machine. They are a butcher's tool, not a mechanic's. True, an "adjustable" can be useful in an emergency, but for workshop maintenance it is best forgotten since, again, the jaws can never be aligned accurately enough to obviate the danger of slipping.

Screwdrivers should have their blades properly ground so that, in side view, the blade is at first concave, and then runs parallel all the way to the tip. This enables it to be seated properly in the slot and to apply its pressure evenly. A screwdriver whose blade is wedge-shaped when viewed from the side cannot seat properly and exerts all its force on the edges of the slot. Understandably, these crumble under the strain, and the screw is useless thereafter.

After use, all tools should be wiped clean, kept in a dry place, and protected from dust by being wrapped in rag. Don't encase them in a plastic bag, for this leads to rusting through excessive condensation. If they are used fairly infrequently they should also be very lightly oiled. The film of lubricant should, of course, be wiped off before they are used again.

# 3 Methodical maintenance

THERE is, obviously, a difference between routine maintenance—the day-to-day adjustments and minor repairs which all vehicles need—and major overhauls, but both have their place in keeping a motor-cycle in good working order.

A motor-cycle invariably repays constant and sympathetic attention to its everyday condition, but certainly does not take kindly to constant stripping of the engine. Oddly, many owners fall into the error of neglecting to give their machines minor attention, while over-conscientiously pulling them apart two or three times each year.

This is the exact opposite of the correct approach. Well driven, and properly maintained, a motor-cycle will cover many miles before a top overhaul (a couple of hours' job) is recommended. Some riders have covered well over 10,000 miles without decarbonizing, but the manufacturers frown on such mileages before the engine is attended to. The machine *can* do it; but should not be asked to.

If the routine maintenance is neglected, however, the time which can elapse between overhauls is drastically shortened and the amount of work needing to be done (and the amount of money which needs to be spent) will be much increased.

The reason for this is simple enough. Maladjustments have a cumulative effect. Little enough harm, for example, will result if a sparking plug is loose and the machine covers 20 miles or so before the fault is discovered. But if, in the absence of a routine check, the loose plug is left for a thousand miles the results can be serious. All sorts of troubles could spring from this one minor example of neglect. Hot gases could burn away the lower threads in the plug hole, and the wobbling plug could elongate the hole itself.

Since the compression would be reduced the engine could never develop its full power, so the performance would fall and the fuel consumption would rise. Extra air drawn in through the plug hole would give a weak mixture, so causing overheating and possible distortion of the barrel and piston. A pretty stiff price, that, for the minute saved by omitting to make a single, simple check.

Or consider the case of the brakes, which gradually deteriorate in their performance. Unless their power and adjustment is constantly checked you may easily find that when an emergency stop has to be made in a distance of forty feet the motor-cycle will not stop in less than forty-five. The result can be very expensive indeed. It is a dangerously unnecessary way of learning a lesson.

## TASK SYSTEMS

Constant and methodical inspection is the best way of preventing troubles, but the usual recommendations, based on elapsed mileage, are difficult to carry out if a full log of the work already done is not kept. For those who wish to follow this system, however, the recommended work is detailed in the Appendix.

This was a problem which faced the Armed Forces some years ago, and to combat it the military authorities evolved "Task Systems," which called for a daily or weekly check on each aspect of the mechanical side of a vehicle.

In a modified form such systems are ideally suited for a privately-owned and maintained motor-cycle. They can be of two types, daily or weekly. Which is used depends entirely on the use to which the motor-cycle is put. If it is a "ride to work" machine checks should be made each day. If it is employed solely for week-end excursions a weekly basis can be substituted.

Taking the daily system first, here is a task system for Suzukis. It is designed to cover all the major parts which need to be checked, but to carry out these recommendations should never involve the expenditure of more than ten minutes in a single day. In most cases, in fact, only a couple of minutes will be needed.

### Daily Task Systems

*Sunday:* check the adjustment of front and rear brakes; check freedom of action of brake controls; check security of nuts and bolts in braking system; check lubrication of brake cables.

*Monday:* check gearbox oil level; check all controls for free movement and adequate lubrication.

*Tuesday:* check all exposed electrical wiring for signs of abrasion or fracture; check all electrical terminals for tightness; check operation of horn, lamps and dip-switch; check contact-breaker setting.

*Wednesday:* examine tyre treads and remove any trapped stones; check tyre pressures; check wheels for security; rock wheels and front fork to check play in bearings.

*Thursday:* check clutch cable for adjustment; check that clutch plates are freeing.

*Friday:* check all accessible nuts and bolts for security; check petrol flow.

*Saturday:* check sparking plug for gap and condition; check battery.

### Alternative Weekly Systems

*Week One:* check gearbox oil level; check plug for gap and condition.

*Week Two:* check brakes for adjustment, freedom and control action, and lubrication of cables; check wheels for security; rock wheels and front fork to check play in bearings; examine tyre treads and adjust pressures.

*Week Three:* examine all electrical leads for signs of abrasion or fracture check all terminals for security; check operation of horn, lamps and dip-switch; check contact-breaker setting.

*Week Four:* check clutch cable for adjustment; check that clutch plates are freeing; check all accessible nuts and bolts for security; check battery.

By employing this approach to routine maintenance of the Suzuki, the rider ensures that most of the major points are checked by the daily system at least once each week. Even allowing for a pretty substantial mileage each day this should mean, at the worst, that no fault could be undetected for more than, say 300 miles. In practice, most defects would be discovered well before they had time to develop to serious proportions.

With the weekly system, a month could elapse between the beginning of a fault and its discovery. Where the machine is used only for a 50-mile week-end jaunt this would be neither here nor there, and so the weekly system would be adequate. If the utilization of the machine is more intense than this, however, settle for daily checks instead.

It is important to remember that the idea is to *check* the relevant points. In nine cases out of ten no adjustment will be necessary: you are only examining the component to find out if it needs to be touched. There is no point in adjusting for its own sake, and where everything is in order you merely leave well alone and pass on to the next point on the list.

Neither system takes into account periodic oil changing and greasing, which still must be carried out on the elapsed mileage basis recommended by the manufacturers. It is all too easy to forget just when the job was last done, and a useful aid to memory in this department is to stick a piece of self-adhesive tape to the parts concerned, noting on the tape the mileage at which the work was last done, or the mileage at which it should next be done. It is a matter of personal preference which scheme you adopt, but don't get the figures mixed up. Mark it boldly "Greased at x miles" or "Next oil change at x miles."

A word of warning, here, about grades of oil and greases. Your handbook lists certain grades of lubricant which should be used, and this is reproduced in the Appendix. The manufacturers do not pick these names out of a hat; nor do they suggest them because they get a "rake-off" from the oil companies. They don't!

The factory and the research departments of the oil companies both carry out long and expensive tests with the various components, using a wide range of oils and greases. The brands which give the best results—longest life with the least wear—are the brands which are eventually recommended. So stick to them, and do not be tempted to use a different grade of lubricant because it is cheaper or because you have read in an advertisement that it has some magical properties. It may well have them —but unless they happen to be the right properties for your particular machine the results may not be as pleasant as you think.

## TOP OVERHAULS

One form of routine maintenance which has been raised almost to the level of a panacea is the top overhaul—a "decoke." Before oils improved so much this was true, but today decarbonizing is necessary only at quite long intervals for the simple reason that modern lubricants do not foul the engine as the old ones did. Once a year or every 4,000 miles is ample. But remember that the tailpipe *must* be detached from the silencer and cleaned at the same time.

To carry out a "decoke," first clean the outside of the engine. Have ready a scraper made by filing the end of a stick of hard solder to a chisel shape; a wire brush; an old screwdriver; a length of discarded bicycle chain; some petrol in which to wash parts; and a stiff-bristled brush.

Detach the silencing system and the cylinder head. You will find details of this work in the specialized chapters. Do not disturb the barrel. Where this is mounted on studs, it pays to slip a pair of distance pieces on to two of the studs and replace a couple of head nuts finger-tight to hold it.

Dismantle the exhaust system by freeing the pipe from the silencer body, and taking the tail pipe out of the end. It is held by a screw, and when this is removed the pipe can be pulled out with pliers.

Start your "decoke" by setting the piston at T.D.C. and scraping all the carbon off the head. You can if you like leave a ring of carbon round the edge to act as an oil and pressure seal. The best way of doing this is to insert an old piston ring on to the crown to act as a template. When the crown is clean, you can finish the job with a little metal polish if you wish.

Now bring the piston to B.D.C. and, working through the stub end, scrape all the carbon out of the exhaust port. Any which enters the cylinder will simply rest on top of the piston, and can be washed away with petrol when you have finished.

Now scrape the carbon out of the head, again finishing off either with the wire brush or with metal polish. Be careful to ensure that the sparking plug hole is free of carbon as well.

The tailpipe can be poked clear with the old screwdriver you used on the exhaust port. If it is badly choked, get a garage to burn away the fouling with a gas torch. An obstructed exhaust can rob you of half your power. Thread the bicycle chain through the pipe itself, and see-saw it back and forth to cut away carbon in the bend.

And that is that. All you need do now is to wipe the bore with oil so that you do not have a "dry" start, and reassemble the parts. Every other time, however, you will have to lift the barrel and inspect the rings. These may have become gummed in their grooves. In this case, the rings must be eased out and a piece of broken piston ring used as a scraper to clear their grooves completely. Obviously, the piston should be removed for this, and while it is off you can check for carbon *inside* the crown. It sometimes forms here as a result of the action of heat.

Do not overdo top overhauls. The engine takes time to settle down after being even partially stripped, and too-frequent dismantling will hinder, not help, your machine. If it is running sweetly, giving a good performance, and not using excessive petrol then leave it alone—whatever mileage it has covered. If it is not, then something is wrong and you should investigate. But don't regard a "decoke" as a cure-all, because it isn't. It is just one of a number of jobs which help to keep the machine in good fettle.

# 4 Overhauling carburettors

HIGHLY efficient Amal carburettors—made in Britain—are fitted to the Suzuki two-strokes. They are all of needle-valve type—a VM-15 SC on the "50s"; and a VM-17 SC on the 80 c.c. models. A feature of these carburettors is the use of a starter system in place of the more usual choke.

The manner in which this operates should be understood. When the lever on the handlebar is pulled towards the rider while the twistgrip throttle is fully closed, and the engine is turned over, air is drawn through the starter air intake, through a bleed and into the float chamber. At the same time, fuel is drawn through the starter jet to mix with this air, the mixture then passing into the starter air intake, where more air is mixed with it. It then enters the main venturi through an orifice just behind the throttle slide.

For normal idling, with the starter slide raised but the throttle slide almost closed, air enters through the idling channel and is metered by the pilot air screw. This air mixes with fuel rising from the pilot jet to form a richer-than-normal mixture which passes into the venturi from an orifice just below the rear edge of the throttle slide. The strength of this mixture is controlled solely by the setting of the pilot air screw, and can be adjusted by varying the screw's position.

Under normal running conditions air is induced direct into the venturi after passing through the air cleaner. The air flow creates a depression around the main jet orifice, and fuel rises to it through the main jet submerged in the float chamber. To assist in emulsifying the mixture, air is bled through a channel to the needle-jet, entering this through five holes. Therefore, the fuel is already partially atomized when it reaches the venturi, and the process is completed by the high-speed airflow under the throttle valve.

Obviously, an instrument of this type is necessarily of very accurate construction, and any work carried out on it should be both gentle and precise. If it is not, damage is likely to occur and the performance of the machine will be affected.

**Carburettor Removal, M 15 and M 15 D.** The basic method of removal on these models is detailed in the overhaul chapters on pages 42–3. It is normal to remove the carburettor body alone, leaving the throttle and starter slides on their cables. If the slides or the throttle needle require attention they can be detached from the cable by holding the cable while the slide is pushed upwards against spring pressure. The cable nipple can then be disengaged from the slide.

**Carburettor Removal, Suzy Models.** On the Suzy "mokick" the carburettor is enclosed in the frame. To detach it, first remove the rear view mirror on the left handlebar and then move the starter lever assembly as far as it will travel towards the centre of the bars, putting the bars themselves on to full right lock. Pull the throttle cable rearwards, but do not disturb the twist grip.

On the right-hand side of the frame is a small rubber plug, set just behind the legshield. On the opposite side is a larger plug. Remove both of these. Take off the tool compartment and battery covers and remove

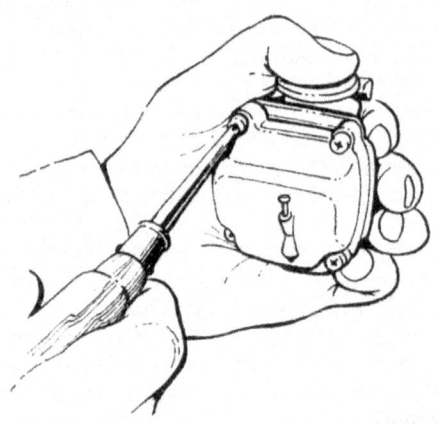

FIG. 15. REMOVING THE FLOAT CHAMBER

To detach the chamber, release the four cross-headed screws which secure it to the main carburettor body.

the battery. Then insert a screwdriver through the hole in the right-hand side of the frame and undo the carburettor clamp screw.

Next, remove the clamp which holds the air cleaner pipe to the intake of the carburettor and pull the pipe clear. You should now be able to ease the instrument off its stub and draw it through the frame aperture.

Unscrew the mixing chamber top and draw out the throttle slide, leaving it attached to the cable unless you wish to remove the slide or needle. In that case proceed as described in the section on the M 15 model. With a 12-mm open-ended spanner, undo the starter plunger nut and draw out the starter plunger assembly, still on its cable. This, again, can be left on the machine unless attention to the cable is required.

**Stripping the Carburettor.** Before carrying out any further work on the carburettor, wipe off all external dirt with a petrol-soaked rag, and dry off the exterior.

Then use a cross-headed screwdriver to remove the four screws at the bottom of the float chamber. Work from one to another diagonally, so avoiding undue stresses. With the screws out the float chamber will pull off (see Fig. 15).

Next, take out the float pin—this simply lifts out of its seating—and

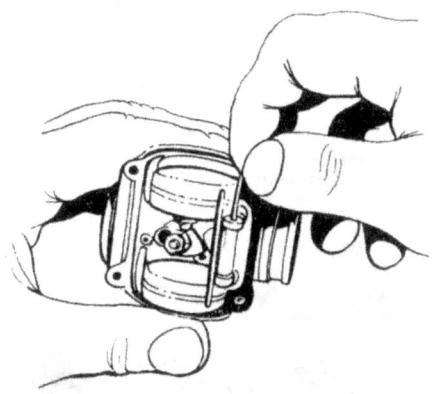

Fig. 16. Detaching the Carburettor Float

The float is held in position merely by a single pin, which can be pulled out with the fingers. Do not drop the float, which is of delicate construction.

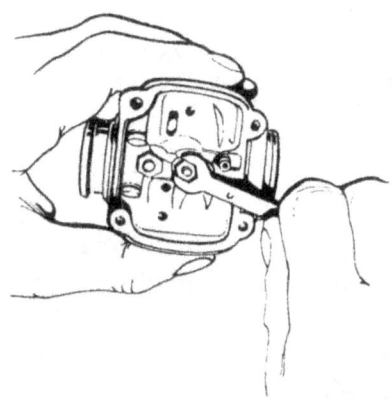

Fig. 17. Detaching the Main Jet

The main jet is screwed into the end of the needle-jet, and can be undone by use of a spanner. Be careful not to strip the thread on replacing it.

detach the twin float unit (see Fig. 16). The main jet is set centrally in the unit and can be undone by use of a 6-mm spanner (see Fig. 17), while the needle-jet into which it is screwed requires an 8-mm spanner. If only the main jet is to be taken out hold the needle-jet steady while the other is being undone.

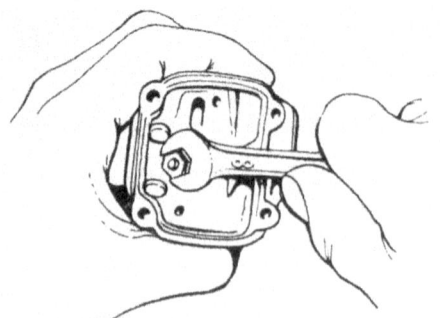

FIG. 18. NEEDLE-VALVE SEATING REMOVAL

The seating for the needle valve will only require detaching if it has been damaged or is badly worn.

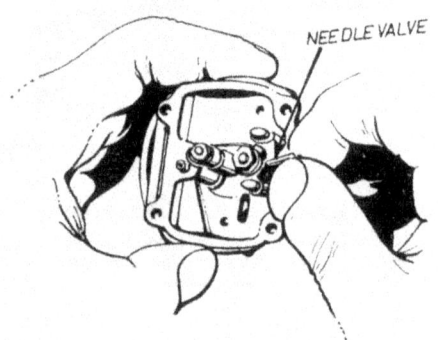

FIG. 19. NEEDLE VALVE REMOVAL

After the float pin has been withdrawn and the float lifted away, the needle valve will drop out of its seating.

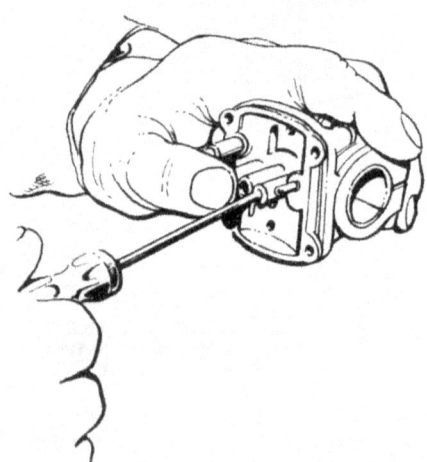

FIG. 20 REMOVAL OF PILOT JET

A thin-bladed screwdriver inserted into the pilot jet channel is used to undo the jet.

## CARBURETTORS

The needle valve which controls admission of fuel from the pipe can be unscrewed with an 8-mm spanner (*see* Figs. 18 and 19) and the pilot jet—set inside the casting just forward of the main jet—is unscrewed with a screwdriver (*see* Fig. 20).

The throttle slide and starter plunger are detached from their cables as

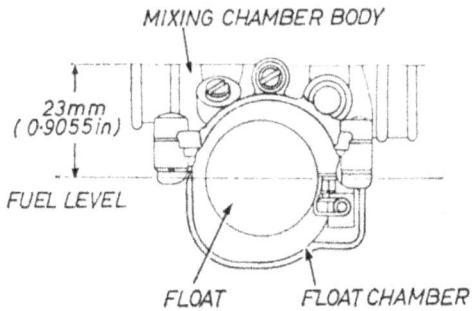

Fig. 21. Fuel Level

Check whether or not the fuel in the float chamber is at the correct level by measuring the distance shown here. It is easiest to do this with the carburettor inverted.

already described, and the needle is freed from the slide by lifting it out on its circlip. The carburettor is now stripped.

**Adjusting the Fuel Level.** Obviously, the performance of the carburettor depends to a considerable extent upon the level of the fuel in the float

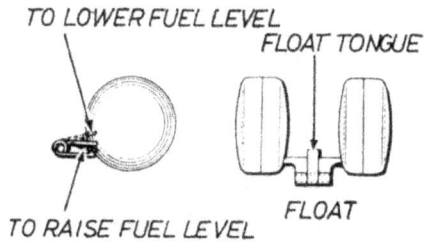

Fig. 22. Adjusting the Fuel Level

The level of fuel in the float chamber can be regulated by bending the needle-valve operating tongue on the float as shown here.

chamber. This should be 23 mm (0·9055 in.) below the centre line of the mixing chamber body (*see* Fig. 21). When the float reaches this point it should cause the needle valve to shut off the supply completely.

The setting may be checked by removing the carburettor, taking off the float chamber, and inverting the instrument. Lift the float, and then lower it gradually. When the float tongue touches the upper end of the needle valve, stop and measure the distance between the carburettor body lip on which the float seats and the lower edge of the float. It should be 22·5 mm (0·8858 in.). Where it is less than this the float is permitting too high a fuel level, and the float tongue should be bent gently to the needle valve side. Then recheck your readings, and adjust again if necessary. Where the distance is more than 22·5 mm the level in the float chamber is too low and the tongue must be bent away from the needle valve (*see* Fig. 22).

**Cleaning Jets.** The only correct way to clean the very fine jets used in this type of carburettor is to wash them in petrol and poke any obstruction clear with a bristle. Metal—such as wire—should not be used, since even slight scratching can alter the capacity of such tiny jets as these.

In fact, jets become worn in use, owing to the fact that fuel contains hundreds of tiny but hard specks of grit, etc. After 10,000 miles have been covered, therefore, it is good policy to fit a completely new set of jets and to use a new needle and slide. The needle valve, too, will need renewal, since this tends to become ridged around the contact area and will no longer provide a good seal. It is easy enough to check this point. Refit the needle valve, connect the fuel pipe, and turn on the fuel while pressing the valve upwards by pressure on the float. If fuel seeps from the valve it is not sealing as it should.

When replacing jets, etc., remember that the material of the carburettor body is a relatively soft casting—so beware of over-tightening. They should seat firmly, but no undue strain should be applied. This will obviate any danger of the jets being distorted, too.

**Carburettor Reassembly.** As with most mechanical components, reassembly is little more than the stripping procedure in reverse. There are, however, one or two points to note.

A new gasket should always be used around the float chamber rim, and like all carburettor gaskets it should be fitted dry. Oil and sealing compounds should not be used, since they tend to squeeze out under pressure and can then block the jets.

Where a new needle is to be used, press the spring circlip out of its groove on the old one and press it on to the new. It should go in the third groove from the top. The needle is then slipped into the slide, the cable is pulled through the mixing chamber top, and the spring is placed over it. With a little manipulation the nipple can be fixed in the slide, and the spring seated home. Operate the throttle once or twice to ensure that all is in order, and then replace the slide in the mixing chamber. Don't force it if it will not enter cleanly. The slot in its side must engage with the guide peg in the body, and the needle must enter the jet. If the slide sticks, one or both of these has not happened, and you must withdraw it and line it up properly. When it is correctly set it will slide in easily.

**Tuning the Carburettor.** When the instrument is back on the machine, the running adjustments can be carried out. First, the idling is set. Ensure that the throttle cable has 0·5–1·0 mm play (0·02–0·04 in.) varying this by means of the adjuster in the cable if it is incorrect. Then start the engine, and allow it to warm up by running it for two or three minutes.

Then screw in the throttle stop screw until the engine speeds up. Slowly turn the pilot air screw inwards until the revs. decrease to the slowest speed at which the engine will run. You can determine this by oscillating the screw slightly. As it is closed the engine will tend to cut; as it is opened the motor will begin to speed up. Leave the screw set so that you are getting just a little more than minimum engine speed at that particular throttle setting—higher than normal, of course, because the throttle slide

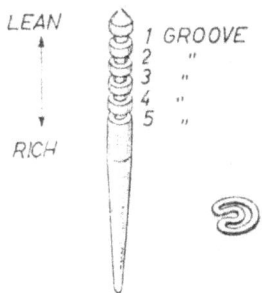

FIG. 23. THE THROTTLE NEEDLE

Richer or leaner mixtures are usually obtained by varying the position of the needle in the slide. It has five grooves in which the circlip can be placed.

has been deliberately set high. Now rack off the throttle stop screw, very slowly, until the engine is running just above its cut-off speed (about 1,200 r.p.m.).

It now remains to get the smoothest possible running. This is done by fine adjustment of the pilot air screw, which should be rotated no more than three-quarters of a turn in either direction. The correct setting will lie within this compass.

High-speed adjustment depends upon the main jet, which controls the performance at openings above three-quarter throttle. If the engine runs more smoothly when the throttle is backed off from fully open the indications are that the mixture is weak. If, on the other hand, the engine speed drops when the throttle is closed slightly it means that the mixture is either correct or, if anything, too rich. Lean mixtures can be corrected by using a larger main jet than the standard 120.

At medium speeds the mixture strength is controlled by the position of the needle in the jet (*see* Fig. 23) and by the throttle slide cutaway, which admits or excludes air according to the depth of the chamfer in its front face.

To adjust by means of the needle, first take a careful note of the colour of the smoke from the exhaust. White smoke suggests an over-rich mixture, and lowering the needle by one notch so that the clip rests in the second groove from the top should cure it.

If, on the other hand, there is no white smoke and the engine seems to be holding back—almost as if the brakes were partly applied—you have a weak mixture and should try raising the needle one notch, so that the clip is in the fourth groove from the top.

In standard form, the carburettor is equipped with a slide having a 1-mm (0·04-in.) cutaway. It is possible to use slides with different cutaways (*see* Fig. 24) to obtain alternative mixtures, but it is not generally

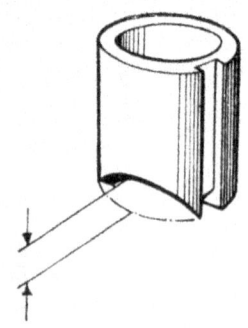

FIG. 24. THE THROTTLE SLIDE

The amount of air admitted by the throttle slide is governed by the depth of the cutaway. By substituting a different slide a degree of mixture control is possible.

thought advisable. Normally, the carburettor will respond to tuning of the needle and the pilot jet, and if it is still not right afterwards the fault is probably elsewhere.

Where you wish to experiment with slides, however, note that one with a larger cutaway gives a weaker mixture, while one with a smaller cutaway will richen it. Unfortunately, the change of cutaway may also affect the slow-running performance.

**Air Filter.** It should not be forgotten that the condition of the air filter also determines whether or not the carburation is correct. A choked element cuts the amount of air reaching the carburettor, and, therefore, richens the mixture all the way through the range. For this reason, it is essential to observe the maker's stipulation that the filter should be cleaned every 1,900 miles.

To do so, detach the right-hand frame cover and take out the battery. On the M 30 the cleaner is mounted alongside the frame; on the motorcycles it is inside it. In the former case it is held by two nuts, and in the latter by a single screw. Release the fastening and—on the motor-cycles —take off the carburettor cover and release the filter pipe clamp. The filter is then lifted from the machine. Motor-cycle filters have a cover, which is freed by removing the holding screws.

# CARBURETTORS

Cleaning is the same in all cases. The filter element is tapped to free the loose dirt, and is brushed with a stiff but dry brush. Under no circumstances should oil or petrol be used on it. Nor should it be washed in water. You can, however, employ blasts from an air line or a vacuum cleaner to remove more dirt. When the filter is absolutely clean, refit it. Where constant carburation troubles are experienced, try the effect of using a brand-new element.

**Fuel Tap.** If weak mixtures are encountered, check that the strainer in the fuel tap filter is not blocked. The tap has a sludge-trap type of

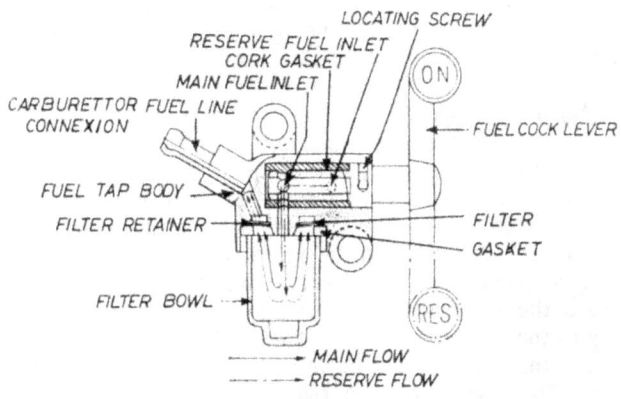

FIG. 25. THE FUEL TAP

An often-overlooked component, the fuel tap must be kept in good condition if maximum economy is to be obtained. Pay particular attention to the security of the joints.

filter, and the bowl is simply unscrewed from the tap by use of a 9-mm spanner, the filter element removed and washed in petrol, and the interior of the bowl cleaned. Use a new gasket on reassembly to ensure that the joint is fuel-tight (*see* Fig. 25).

# 5 Electrical overhauls

ON all the smaller Suzuki models, electrical current for the ignition and lighting systems is drawn from a flywheel magneto or from a generator which "doubles" as an electric starter. How these components should be removed from the machine is described in the relevant engine overhaul chapters. Generally speaking, removal should be necessary only during a complete engine strip, although the flywheel must come off magneto-equipped models for the replacement of the contact-breaker or coils.

**Contact-breaker Removal.** A contact-breaker is merely a switch operated by a cam. It is in two parts—a fixed contact carried on a plate screwed to the stator; and a moving contact carried on a centre-pivotted arm. To detach the contact-breaker unit, remove the left-hand crankcase cover and, on magneto models, draw off the flywheel rotor.

Detach the contact-breaker from the stator by removing the clamping screw from the fixed plate. This will enable the unit to be pulled away. Then release the nut and bolt carrying the electrical lead. Note the positioning of the washers, lead terminal and leaf spring before you do so. It is essential that they should be refitted in exactly the same places on reassembly, otherwise there is a risk of short-circuiting the magneto. The bolt and the leaf spring *must* be insulated from the fixed plate, otherwise the unit will not work.

With the removal of the lead the contact-breaker is free from the machine and can be stripped.

**Stripping the Contact-breaker.** Loosening the nut and bolt for the lead will have freed one end of the leaf spring. To detach the moving contact arm, therefore, merely requires that the securing circlip should be pressed out of its slot on the pivot post, and the arm lifted upwards. Here, again, be careful to note the positioning of all washers, since the post forms part of the contact plate and the arm must be insulated from it.

**Truing the Points.** With the contact-breaker stripped, each point in turn can be trued-up on a stone. The aim should be to get it absolutely true, with the contact surface square and unpitted. If the points are badly worn it is better to fit a completely new contact-breaker set.

**Refitting the Contact-breaker.** Assembling and replacing the unit is, again, simply removal and stripping in reverse and should present no problems.

**Gapping the Contact-breaker.** After removal—and periodically during service—the contact-breaker points gap will have to be reset. On magnetoed machines it is done through the access holes in the flywheel; but on starter-equipped models the breaker is fully exposed when the left-hand engine cover has been removed.

To check the gap (0·3–0·4 mm = 0·012–0·016 in. on all models) remove the sparking plug from the cylinder head and turn the engine until the points are seen to be fully open. Then measure the gap with a feeler gauge, aiming to obtain a setting of 0·35 mm (0·014 in.). If the gap is outside the limits of plus or minus two thousandths' of an inch of this "ideal" setting, loosen the screw which clamps the fixed plate to the stator (*see* Fig. 26).

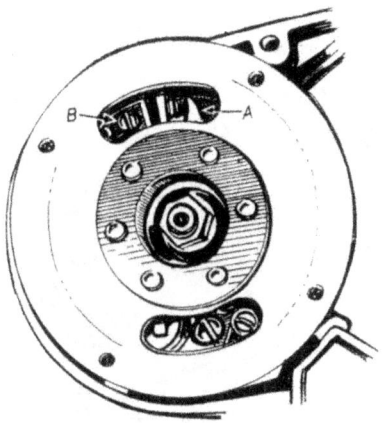

FIG. 26. CHECKING THE CONTACT-BREAKER GAP

The contact-breaker points "*A*" can be seen through the window in the flywheel face. If adjustment is required the screw "*B*" is slightly loosened to enable the contact plate to be moved.

Do not undo it. It is essential that the plate should be able to move only against friction. On the plate is a slot, in which a screwdriver must be inserted. On magneto models it is just above the lead terminal; on starter-equipped machines on the outer edge of the plate. By turning the screwdriver to the right the gap between the points can be narrowed, and by turning it to the left it can be increased.

When the correct gap has been obtained, leave the feeler in place and clamp down the fixing screw. Then recheck the gap, using first the 0·014-in. feeler, then feelers 0·002-in. larger and smaller to ensure that you have a setting which is within the permitted tolerance.

**Cleaning the Points.** In use, the contact points become dirty and burned. Once or twice a year it is advisable to clean them. This is best done by using a special contact points file, which is inserted into the space between the points and used to cut away the damaged surfaces. Then, a final clean can be given by inserting a piece of clean postcard between the points, closing them on to it so that they rub against it, and withdrawing it smartly. Do this repeatedly, until the card comes away clean.

After filing and cleaning, the points gap must, of course, be reset, since any material which has been burned off the contact surfaces (and any which has been cut away by filing) will have enlarged the gap between them.

**Re-timing the Ignition (Flywheel Magneto Models).** Remove the gear lever and the left-hand crankcase cover to give unobstructed access to the magneto. Remove the flywheel nut, using a 14-mm box spanner, and then

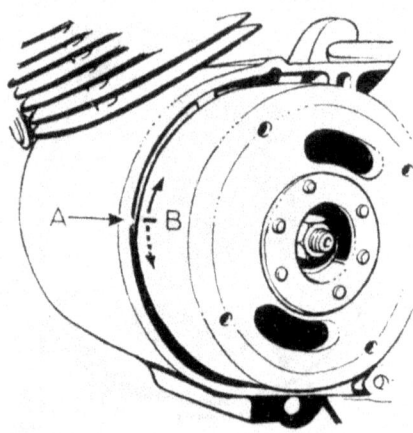

FIG. 27. IGNITION TIMING MARKS

For the timing to be correct, the points should be breaking when the pip "*A*" and the line "*B*" coincide. To advance the ignition the stator must be moved in the direction of the solid arrow. To retard it, move it in the direction of the dotted arrow.

turn the flywheel round slowly. Watch the contact points all the time, and stop rotating the flywheel at the instant the points begin to break. The line scribed on the flywheel should now be in line with the pip formed on the inner front lip of the crankcase (*see* Fig. 27). This is the correct firing point—27° B.T.D.C. If the line is above the pip the ignition is retarded. If it is below it, the ignition is over-advanced. In either case, it should be readjusted.

Without rotating the crankshaft, fit the extractor and draw off the flywheel. Then loosen the three screws which hold the stator plate to the crankcase (*see* Fig. 28), and turn the plate until the points are just breaking. Where the ignition was retarded the plate must be turned anti-clockwise to open the points earlier. If it was over-advanced, it must be turned clockwise to delay opening. When the setting is correct, re-tighten the stator screws and refit the flywheel. Do not tighten its nut at this stage, however. First carry out the timing check once again to make absolutely certain that the setting is right. If it is, the centre nut may be tightened and the cover and gear lever replaced.

**Re-timing the Ignition (Starter-equipped Models).** The routine is basically similar to that just described, except that the marks to be aligned are notches—one on the cam and one on the stator—set at about four o'clock on the plate. With these aligned the points should just be breaking.

To adjust, loosen the two slotted screws which hold the contact-breaker

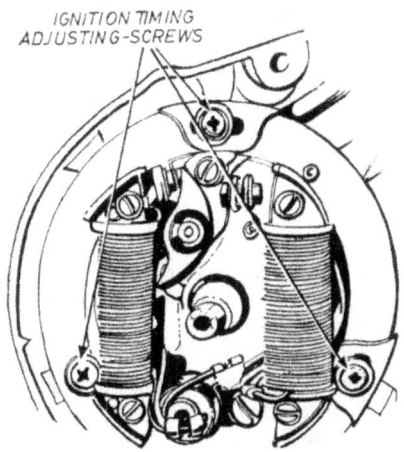

FIG. 28. STATOR PLATE SCREWS

These are the three screws which secure the stator plate, and which must be loosened before any adjustment can be made to the ignition timing.

assembly, and insert a screwdriver into the uppermost notch on the plate. Move the breaker plate until the points are just opening. Turning the plate clockwise will advance the ignition, and turning it anti-clockwise will retard it. When the setting is correct, lock up the screws again, rotate the crankshaft once more to bring the marks into alignment, and make a further check on the timing.

**Re-timing Without Dismantling.** Within strict limits, the timing can be adjusted simply by varying the gap between the points. Where the ignition is retarded, opening the gap to a maximum of 0·4 mm (0·016 in.) will correct it. If it is advanced, closing them to a minimum of 0·3 mm (0·012 in.) will rectify matters. Outside these limits, the full re-timing procedure is required.

**Sparking Plug Care.** Two-strokes are very sensitive indeed to the condition of the sparking plug. It must be of the right grade for the job the machine is doing and it must be in good order. Also, it must be correctly gapped.

Plugs are sometimes referred to as "hot" and "cold." This refers to their own ability to withstand oiling. A "hot" plug runs hotter and thus burns up oil which would foul a "cold" plug. The latter, on the other hand, can operate under combustion-chamber conditions which would burn out the "hot" plug. A list of suitable plugs for the Suzuki is given in the Appendix, and you should be sure that your machine is using one of them.

The gap between the points must be set to 0·5–0·6 mm (0·020–0·024 in.) and the plug should be checked regularly—say, at 500-mile intervals. If it is dirty, have it cleaned on a garage sand-blaster. This is the only really satisfactory method. Wire brushes will not remove all the encrusted dirt, and there is a risk that minute traces of metal from the brush will be deposited on the insulator nose, leading to tracking and consequent loss of some of the H.T. current.

Sparking plugs are cheap—in fact, their price has not varied since 1936! It pays, therefore, to fit new plugs frequently. Even in a water-cooled car engine a plug will last for only 10,000 miles before its efficiency is seriously affected. In a hard-working air-cooled two-stroke unit, replacement after a maximum of 5,000 miles is a wise precautionary measure.

When fitting a sparking plug, make sure that the threads are clean but do not oil or grease them—lubricant carbonizes under heat and you may make the plug difficult to remove by using it. It is essential that the copper sealing washer should not be omitted, and if the one on your plug is flattened it should be discarded and a new one fitted. Garages can supply new ones at a cost of a few pence. Tighten the plug only enough to half crush the washer, and deny yourself the luxury of that final jerk on the plug spanner. It can result in over-tightening the threads and possibly in distorting the plug body too. When that happens you may get an air leak into the cylinder, with its associated bogy of weak mixtures, hot running, and eventual seizure.

**Plug Cap.** The sparking plug cap is fitted to the H.T. lead by means of an integral screw which enters the conducting core. If this joint is not tight it can cause arcing, which will eventually eat away the metal of the pin. Apparent total ignition failure can sometimes be traced to a broken contact at this point.

Whenever the plug is removed for cleaning, wipe the inner surfaces of the cap with clean rag to remove any road dirt which has settled there. If it contains metallic traces it can cause tracking and misfiring in wet weather.

Bad contact in the cap can often be cured simply by unscrewing it (anti-clockwise) from the lead, cutting a quarter of an inch or so off this, and then replacing the cap so that the screw bites into new conductor core.

**Ignition Faults.** The time-honoured test when the motor will not start or when it stops is to take off the plug cap, hold the bare H.T. lead about an eighth of an inch away from a convenient head nut, switch on the ignition and operate the kick starter. If a fat blue spark leaps from the lead to the nut, it indicates that either the sparking plug is faulty (try the engine with a new plug) or that the gap is wrong.

No spark at all—or only a weakish red spark—suggests that the contact-breaker points are burned, pitted, or badly set. If the points pass muster, however, a coil fault is probable. This means a garage test, unless you have spare coils which could be substituted. Another possibility when there is no spark is that the condensor is faulty. If its leads are broken the contact points will be badly burned as well.

A rarer ignition fault is loss of flywheel magnetism—again, a job for the garage. This can be caused by a faulty selenium rectifier, allowing the flow of current to be reversed. When that happens, it flows from the battery to the magneto and de-magnetizes the rotor. Where this fault has been encountered, it is essential that the rectifier should be properly tested too.

**Charging Circuit.** No adjustments are possible on the charging circuit. Electricity for charging the battery is supplied from the lighting coil on the stator. When the machine is in use at night, this current feeds the headlamp direct, delivering between six volts and 7·5 volts according to engine speed. When the lights are not in use the current feeds only the battery, through the selenium rectifier. This converts it into direct current. At 4,000 r.p.m. it gives a charge of over 0·4 amp., dropping to 0·3 amp. at 8,000 r.p.m.

**Battery Care.** In use, the battery loses some of the water from its electrolyte, and this must be replenished until the electrolyte level is within the limits marked on the battery case. Use only distilled water for this. Tap water, rain water, etc., may all contain impurities which would harm the plates.

You can buy distilled water from a chemist for a matter of a few pence —but take your own screw-top bottle for it. It can be transferred into thirsty cells most easily by means of suction. Bare the battery, and take off the filler plugs. Insert a short length of polythene tubing—of a diameter small enough to fit into the battery filler orifices—into your bottle of distilled water. Place your thumb hard over the end of the tube, and a quantity of distilled water will be drawn into the other end. Transfer this to the battery (it will stay in the tube until you take your thumb off the top, thanks to suction) repeating until the level is correct. Then pass on to the next cell.

Keep all battery connexions tight and clean. If corrosion sets in around terminal posts, combat it by applying a strong solution of soda bicarbonate. This is alkaline, and it will neutralize the acid deposits. After treatment, smear petroleum jelly (Vaseline) over the posts, etc. This is a good conductor of electricity so it will not have any harmful side effects.

**Specific Gravity.** The state of charge of a battery is verified by measuring the specific gravity of the electrolyte. This should be done with a hydrometer, whose tube is inserted into each cell in turn (*see* Fig. 29). A little of the electrolyte is sucked into the instrument, whose body contains a float. According to the position of this float in the electrolyte, so the specific gravity varies. It is read off on a scale on the float itself, holding the hydrometer at eye level.

Normally, a fully charged battery will give a reading of 1·260 or better on each cell. A specific gravity of 1·230 indicates a three-quarter charged

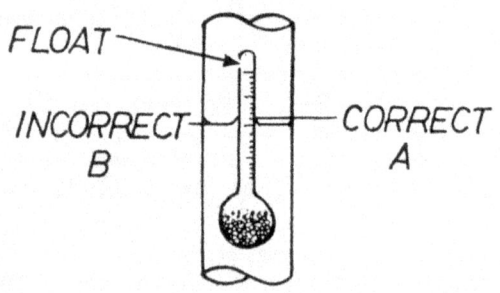

FIG. 29. READING A HYDROMETER

When checking the specific gravity of the battery, take the reading at the point "*A*" where the fluid touches the float; not on the meniscus at point "*B*."

battery; 1·200 a half-discharged one; 1·170 a three-quarter discharged cell; 1·140 almost no charge; and 1·110 no charge at all.

Specific gravity readings should never be taken immediately after topping up with distilled water, and it should be noted that they vary with heat. At freezing point a fully charged cell will register 1·274; at a temperate 68°F it will read 1·260; and at 86°F the reading will be 1·253.

**Battery Troubles.** Most battery troubles are irreparable. All one can do is to fit a new battery in place of the old one. These maladies include the loss of plate material from the positive plates (*see* Fig. 30). This drops to the bottom of the case as a sediment, decreasing battery capacity. It is caused by excessive charging and discharging, and if one does not want the new battery to go the dismal way of the old it is essential that the cause should be found and rectified. Only an auto-electrician can do this.

The same applies to warpage of the positive plates, which results from over-discharging; and to a battery short-circuit due to excessive charging and discharging. Use at high temperatures—the other main cause of this type of failure—is unlikely to be encountered in the British Isles.

Shrinkage of the negative plates or fouling of the separators are two further irremediable faults. In the first instance the battery will accept a charge, but loses capacity quickly; in the latter, the separators become brittle and fail. The first fault is caused by repeated high discharges and repeated overcharging; the latter by high temperatures or too high a specific gravity. It can also occur as a result of plate warpage.

Sulphation of the negative plates—if slight—can be rectified by a long charge at a very low rate. You can recognize this condition by several symptoms—white dots appearing on the plates; and a drop in specific gravity and in battery capacity. The causes include leaving the battery too long without a charge, letting the plates become exposed, and contamination in the electrolyte. With bad sulphation a new battery will, again, be required.

**Access to Bulbs.** Bulbs do not have an indefinite life—an average of around 1,500 hours is normal. Access to them for replacement is pretty

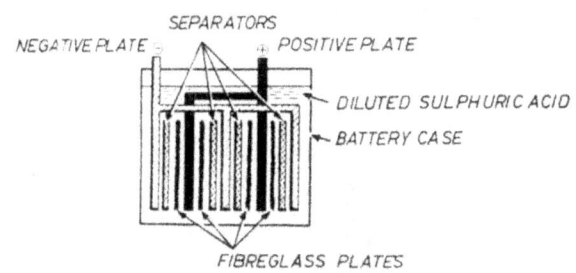

Fig. 30. How the Battery is Constructed
A cross-section through a typical lead-acid battery, showing the disposition of the plates.

straightforward: in the case of the tail and indicator lamps, the lens is removed by undoing its securing screws when the bulb is readily accessible. With the headlamp, the reflector assembly is removed by undoing the large cross-headed screw at the bottom of the lamp, lifting the entire lens/reflector unit, and then detaching the bayonet-fitting headlamp socket from the rear of the reflector. The speedometer bulb can be reached in the same way, simply by pulling on its holder when the headlamp unit has been detached.

**Headlamp Adjustment.** The "throw" of the headlamp beam is set by means of the adjuster screw located in the lower run of the headlamp rim. Screwing in the adjuster raises the beam; racking it off lowers it. This adjustment should be carried out with the engine running—the headlamp will not operate otherwise—and the machine on its wheels with the rider aboard.

**Switchgear.** Nothing can be done—or should be done—to the switches other than to give them a little lubrication from time to time. In the case of the ignition switch, oil can be run on to the tumblers by wetting the ignition key with lubricant and inserting it into the switch. By moving it in and out, and turning the switch with it, the internals can be kept lubricated and protected against damp.

Before and after each winter, remove the tops of the handlebar switches (*see* Fig. 31) by freeing the screws which clamp the two halves together and run a little light oil on to the springs and pivots. Do not overdo this. It is enough just to moisten them.

The neutral indicator switch, being fully enclosed, needs no attention. The brake lamp switch can, however, benefit if the exposed linkage is

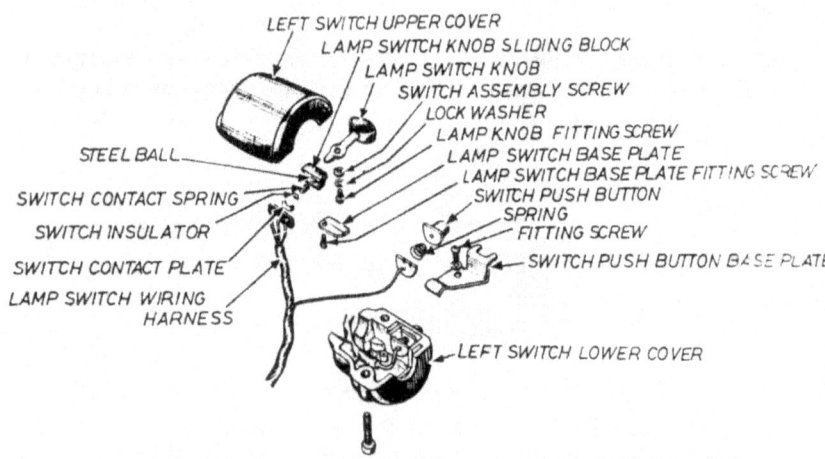

FIG. 31. HANDLEBAR SWITCH LAYOUT
This is how the switch built into the left handlebar grip is arranged. That on the opposite handlebar is of similar construction.

lubricated periodically with engine oil. It should also be correctly set, so that the lamp will light when the brake pedal still requires a bare quarter-inch of travel before it is fully depressed. To do so, loosen the adjusting nuts on the switch body and move it up or down until the required setting is found. Then lock up both nuts carefully.

# 6 Renovating the 50 c.c. motor-cycle engines

BOTH the M 15 and M 15D Suzuki engines are straightforward two-strokes of quite conventional design and layout, and, therefore, the tackling of a complete overhaul is within the compass of the owner who has an average knowledge of workshop procedures and who possesses a tool kit of the type set out in Chapter 2.

**Preparatory Work.** Before you begin to strip the mechanism it is essential to remove all dirt from the outside of the unit as a precaution. This will have a two-fold advantage. It will not only ensure against the chance of grit finding its way on to the delicate internal working surfaces, but it will also make the whole task cleaner to carry out, and, therefore, more enjoyable.

The best method is to brush the outside of the unit thoroughly with a grease solvent, such as Gunk. Make sure that you get it into every nook and cranny, both top and bottom. Work it in with a stiff-bristled brush. After it has had a few minutes in which to soak into the dirt, wash it all away with a gentle flow of water from a hose. Don't blast the water on—it isn't necessary. With a solvent, dirt can be floated off. Finish the job by mopping up any pools of water with an absorbent cloth, and the motor is ready to be worked on.

Place clean newspaper on your workbench—or, if you are using the garage floor, make sure the surface is as clean as possible and then use newspaper to cover an area sufficiently large to enable you to put down all the components you intend to remove. Have ready some clean cardboard boxes—any grocer will be only too happy to supply you with these—in which to place parts after cleaning. For the cleaning itself, have a large baking tin half full of petrol; a stiff-bristled brush (*not* the one you use with grease solvent!); another large tray for draining; and a supply of clean, non-fluffy rag. You are now all set to go, but remember, no cigarettes!

**What Must Come Off?** There are some jobs for which it is essential to lift the engine out of the frame. They are—

Work on the crankshaft; checking or replacing main bearings or oil seals; any work on the gearbox which entails access to the transmission gears; work on the gear-selector cam and its associated mechanism.

Jobs for which the engine can be left in the frame and the appropriate parts removed as necessary are—

Work on such ancillaries as the carburettor and generator; work on the head, barrel, piston and exhaust system; clutch repairs and adjustments; work on the primary transmission.

To avoid repetition, I will describe the work in the form of a complete engine strip—which, of course, involves engine removal. For jobs which can be done without this, merely refer to the sections which apply to the particular work in hand. But do not skimp the preparatory work just because the entire unit is not going to be opened up. Clean, at least, the whole of the area on which you intend to work.

### STRIPPING THE ENGINE

Make sure that the fuel tap is switched off before you begin. Then start the engine and allow it to run until it has used up all the fuel in the float chamber and the fuel line.

Where legshields are fitted, remove them. Each is held by two fastenings.

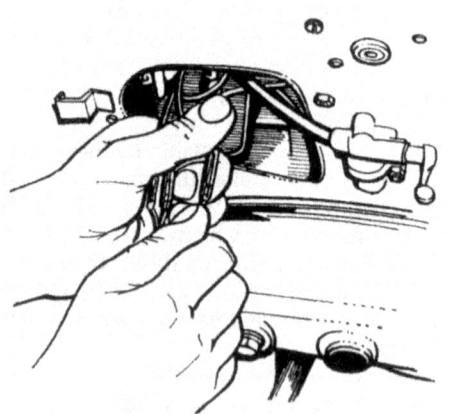

FIG. 32. DISCONNECTING THE WIRING HARNESS

All the wires are colour-coded. For removing the engine, merely undo the snap connectors. When linking them up again, join the appropriately-coloured wires on the engine harness to those on the frame loom.

At the top, there is a nut and spring washer, with two large load-spreading washers set one at each side of the shield. A pair of rubber washers is set similarly at the bottom mounting, loaded against the shielding by means of large steel washers and locked by a through-bolt. Note that the thicker of the rubber washers goes between the shield and the frame while the thinner one is placed between the bolt and the shield. Do not mix them up.

Free the two bolts—one on each shield—which hold the two halves of the carburettor cover. The left-hand bolt is the shorter of the two. When separating these shields, take care not to lose the dowels which hold them together.

The engine is now clear for stripping, which can best be done by working on one side of the machine at a time.

## RENOVATING THE 50 C.C. MOTOR-CYCLE ENGINES

**Work on the Nearside.** This comprises releasing the fuel pipe, throttle slide, starter slide and air cleaner pipe from the carburettor; draining the transmission; removing the gear lever; detaching the left-hand crankcase cover; freeing the drive chain; removing the tool box; and disconnecting the electrical leads (*see* Fig. 32).

**Work on the Offside.** On the right-hand side of the machine, one has to remove the kick starter; detach the exhaust pipe; remove the right-hand crankcase cover; detach the battery box; take off the battery and

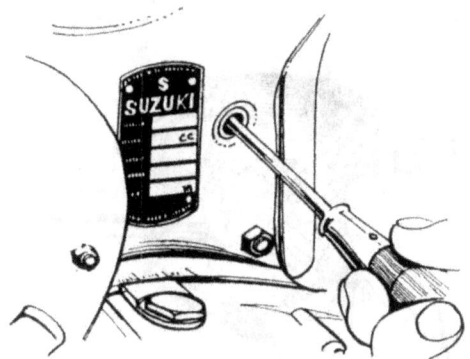

FIG. 33. FREEING THE CARBURETTOR CLAMP SCREW

A rubber plug on the right-hand side of the frame closes the access hole for the clamp screw. Insert a cross-headed screwdriver and loosen it just enough to allow the carburettor to move freely on its stub.

disconnect its cables; free the battery holder; and release the three engine set bolts.

**Disconnecting the Carburettor Controls.** Note that it is permissible, if you wish, to leave the carburettor assembled and simply take it off its stub complete. This entails releasing the spring clip from the rubber pipe on the air cleaner and slipping the connector free of the carburettor. With a screwdriver, loosen the screw on the clamp on the carburettor stub, and slide the entire instrument backwards until it clears the stub. It can then be wired out of the way, using any convenient point on the frame of the machine.

Where you prefer to leave the carburettor body on the engine during removal, first unscrew the large knurled cap on the mixing chamber top and carefully draw out the throttle slide. Do not remove it from its cable. With a spanner, unscrew the starter hexagon, in front and to the right of the mixing chamber, and withdraw the plunger, leaving this, too, still attached to its cable. Wire the two cables to the frame so that both plungers are held safely out of harm's way. Then remove the air cleaner tube, as already described.

**Draining the Oil.** Place a tin under the engine and, using a 23-mm box spanner, undo the drain plug. This is under the right-hand crankcase cover, but owing to the position of the exhaust pipe and foot-brake pedal it is reached more easily from the left-hand side. To obviate the suction effect inside the unit, remove the oil filler plug while the oil is draining away. Afterwards, lightly screw in both plugs for safe keeping.

**Gear Pedal Removal.** Make sure that neutral has been selected. Then scribe a line from the gear selector spindle on to the pedal itself so that

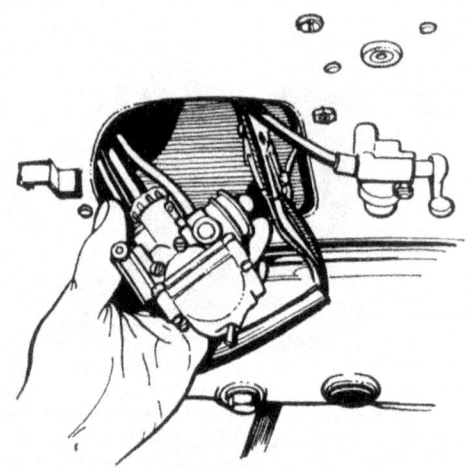

FIG. 34. REMOVING THE M 30 CARBURETTOR

The carburettor on this model is completely enclosed in the frame, and has to be eased out through the access panel on the left-hand side.

you will be able to refit the pedal in the same position without time-wasting juggling with the setting. Using a 10-mm spanner, undo the pinch bolt. Do not lose its small spring washer. The pedal can now be pulled off. If it is stiff on the shaft, free it by inserting a screwdriver into its slot and twisting to spring it open slightly.

**Left-hand Cover Removal.** When stripping the engine there is no need to disturb the small auxiliary cover plate on this side, which is there simply to give easy access to the generator for routine adjustments. Merely free the three screws holding the cover, and pull it away from the engine. If it sticks, gently tap around the cover/crankcase joint with a block of wood to break the seal. Do not insert a screwdriver into the joint to lever it, or you may crack the casing.

**Removing the Driving Chain.** Bring the chain connector link on to the gearbox sprocket by turning the rear wheel. Lever the spring clip off, dismantle the connecting link, and so part the chain.

# RENOVATING THE 50 C.C. MOTOR-CYCLE ENGINES

Have a piece of wire handy and loop this through the end link of the top run of the chain. Tie the ends round the footrest so that the chain is secured. The lower run of the chain can be left hanging.

**Cable Disconnexion.** Remove the tool box and disconnect the cables from the *D*, *F* and *M* terminals on the regulator. This applies to the M 15 D model only. Release the black cable from the ignition switch to the generator and the blue cable to the neutral indicator light at their snap connectors.

**Kickstarter Removal.** The kickstarter is held by a 10-mm pinch bolt. Remove this, and it will pull off its shaft.

**Exhaust Pipe Removal.** The exhaust pipe is held to its flange by two 10-mm nuts. There is also a clamp set just forward of the rubber joint between the pipe and the silencer. Do not disturb this. Its purpose is not to clamp the pipe to the silencer, but to act as a stop for the joint as the two are mated.

To remove the pipe, therefore, just detach the two nuts and their lock washers and pull the pipe forwards until it is clear both of its studs on the head and of the silencer. If the gasket is undamaged it can be used again.

**Right-hand Cover Removal.** If you wish, the offside cover can be left in place until the engine is removed. In this case, release the clutch cable at the handlebar end by pulling the lever back to the bar and then tugging the outer casing free of its stop as the lever is released. The cable is then pulled away from the machine.

If the casing is to be removed leave the clutch cable in position and remove the ring of cross-headed screws which hold the case to the engine. When these are all out, detach the case. If it sticks, tap it around its joint with a hardwood block. It can be left hanging on the clutch cable while the rest of the work is done.

**Battery Removal.** Undo the knurled knob securing the battery box lid. Detach the strap which holds the battery in place. and disconnect the positive and negative cables at their connectors. Lift the battery out and place it well away from the machine, so that it will not get knocked over. Then free the brown engine earthing lead.

**Engine Bolt Removal.** Place wooden blocks—an old wooden box will do admirably—under the engine so that it is supported. Using a 14-mm box spanner, undo the three through-bolts which secure the engine to the frame. Each has a nut, spring washer, and plain washer. Taking the weight of the engine momentarily, press out the bolts. First, work from the right and push out the bottom bolts. Then, from the left, press out the single top bolt (*see* Fig. 35). The engine can now be lifted away from the machine and all further stripping can take place on the workbench.

**Cylinder Head Removal.** Unscrew the sparking plug, using a 21-mm plug spanner. Then, working diagonally (*see* Fig. 36) from side to side, remove the four cylinder head holding-down nuts. For this, a 10-mm box

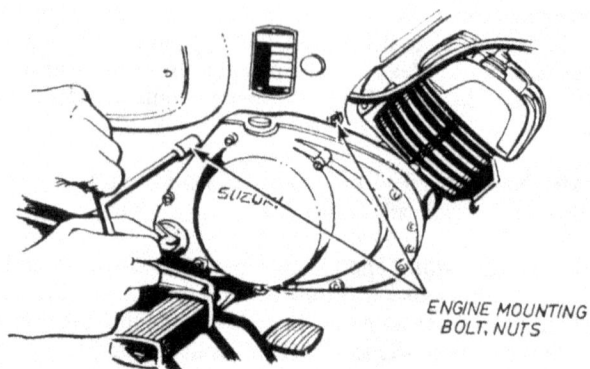

FIG. 35. THE THREE-POINT ENGINE MOUNTING

When detaching the engine from a Suzuki, these are the three main bolts which have to be freed. The engine should be supported from below, and the top bolt removed last of all.

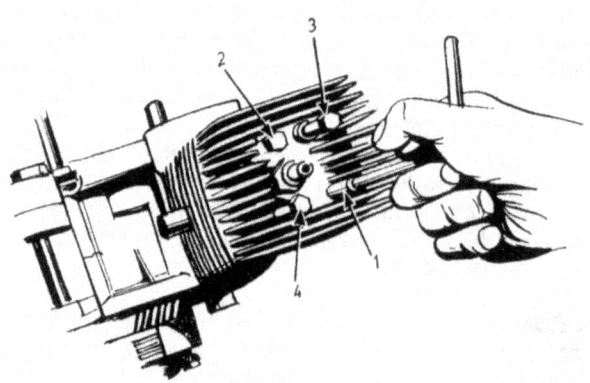

FIG. 36. TIGHTENING THE HEAD NUTS

To avoid distortion, the head nuts must be tightened a little at a time, working from one to another in the sequence shown here. The same sequence applies to the cylinder base nuts on the 80 c.c. models.

spanner is required. Each nut has a flat 6-mm washer. Do not lose these.

The head can now be lifted off the studs. If it is stiff it may be jarred gently with a length of hardwood, but under no circumstances must anything be inserted into the head/cylinder joint in an attempt to lever it off. Distortion of the head and/or damage to the jointing surfaces would result. After the head has been lifted, take off the copper-asbestos gasket. Discard this and fit a new one on reassembly.

**Cylinder Removal.** If the carburettor body was left on the engine, free its clamp and slide it off its stud before removing the cylinder itself. Then turn the crankshaft until the piston is at the bottom of its stroke and gently slide the cylinder barrel off its studs. As the piston emerges from the bottom of the bore support it, so that it cannot fall forwards and be damaged. If the barrel is hard to move, jar the barrel/crankcase joint with a block of hardwood but, again, do not try to insert a lever between the two surfaces or severe damage may be caused.

When lifting the barrel, keep an eye on the gasket inserted between the barrel and the crankcase. It may tend to stick to the barrel on one side and to the case on the other and become torn. If it can be prevented from doing so and is in good condition it can be re-used.

**Checking the Barrel for Wear.** A rough check on cylinder wear can be made by inserting a piston ring squarely into the lower skirt of the barrel and measuring the ring gap. It should be no more than 0·7 mm (0·028 in.). If it is, have the barrel properly checked with internal micrometers to establish whether a rebore is needed.

**Flywheel Removal, M 15.** Prevent the crankshaft rotating by inserting under the piston the special holder tool No. T 036. If you cannot hire one of these from your local agent, blocking up between the lower edges of the piston and the mouth of the crankcase with hardwood strips will give the same result.

Then fix a 14-mm box spanner on to the centre nut of the crankshaft and undo it. Remove the nut and its plain washers, and screw in the flywheel extractor (No. T 032). This has a left-hand thread. With the tool, break the taper and draw off the flywheel, taking care not to lose or damage the Woodruff key which positions it.

**Stator Removal, M 15.** So that you will not "lose" the timing, scribe a mark on the stator plate and on to the crankcase, so that the stator can be refitted in its exact position without difficulty. Then detach the three stator screws, disconnect the neutral indicator lead, and slide the lead-carrying rubber grommets from their crankcase slots. There are two of them. The stator can then be pulled sideways, off the crankcase. It must be placed in the flywheel so that there is no danger of damage.

**Stator Removal, M 15 D.** Lift the brushes, detach the three securing screws, and pull off the stator plate. In this type of unit, the rotor is behind the plate, and cannot be detached while the stator is still in position.

**Rotor Removal, M 15 D.** Lock the crankshaft as described for the M 15 model, and with a 10-mm box spanner undo the rotor securing screw.

Then affix the armature puller (Tool No. T 029) and use this to withdraw the rotor from the shaft.

**Neutral Indicator Switch Removal.** Remove the three cross-headed screws which hold the neutral indicator switch, just above the final drive sprocket. The switch has a paper gasket. Beneath the switch is the contact spring. This is held by a single cross-headed screw with a 6-mm spring washer.

**Drive Sprocket Removal.** Before the nut holding the drive sprocket can be detached the locking tab washer must be flattened, using a suitable drift and a hammer. To prevent the sprocket turning, Tool No. T 044 is used, but it is normally satisfactory to loop a length of chain round the sprocket and pull it up tight to hold it while the nut is freed. The job is done with a 26-mm box or socket spanner. When the nut has been removed the sprocket can be lifted from its splines and the spacer which is set behind it detached. Remember that a new lock washer will be required on reassembly.

**Side Cover Removal.** Where the off-side crankcase cover was left in position it must now be detached by freeing its ring of seven cross-headed screws.

**Kickstarter Return Spring Removal.** Inside the coiled kickstarter spring is a guide or split collar. This is pulled straight out, using a pair of pliers. Then—again with the pliers—pull out the spring itself. One end is tugged straight up from its hole in the kickstarter spindle, the other from the hole in the casing.

A pair of circlip pliers is required to take out the return spring set circlip, which is located in a groove on the spindle. When this has been sprung out of position the return spring holder and washer can be detached.

**Dismantling the Clutch.** Lift the dome-headed push rod and its associated shims out of the centre of the pressure plate. Don't lose the shims—they are there to give the correct clearance between the push rod and the ball in the end of the clutch operating screw.

Now turn the engine on its side and compress the clutch springs so that you can remove the six 5-mm hexagon-headed nuts. For this you will want a 9-mm spanner. Work from one nut to another, diagonally across the clutch. When the nuts and shakeproof washers are all off, take away the pressure plate with its six springs and six cups. Then remove all the clutch plates.

To dismantle the clutch further its hub must be stopped from turning. A special tool (No. T 031) is used here, but blocking the bottom of the piston or inserting a lever across adjacent clutch nut studs should do the trick in its absence. Flatten the tab washer behind the centre nut, apply

# RENOVATING THE 50 C.C. MOTOR-CYCLE ENGINES

a 21-mm box spanner, and tap the tommy bar smartly with a hammer until the nut loosens. Then remove it, and lift away the splined clutch centre, its thrust washer, the main clutch body, and the body's thrust washer.

**Primary Drive Pinion Removal.** Here, again, the crankshaft must be locked by blocking up under the piston or by use of Tool No. T 036. Undo the pinion nut and take off both nut and washer. To remove the pinion itself another special tool is essential. This is the primary pinion puller (Tool No. T 025 A) which is fitted to the teeth of the pinion and hammered round to free the grip of the pinion on its taper.

**Removing the Gearchange Mechanism.** When the selector mechanism is operated, the cam drum is halted at the various gear positions by means of a cam stopper. It is this which is the next part to be removed.

Using a 10-mm box spanner, undo the set screw which holds the stopper. It is set within a small coil spring and spacer, all of which will come away with the stopper.

Next, detach the gearchange shaft circlip and its thrust washer, free the selector arm claws from the drum, and drive out the shaft, together with the selector arm and spring. It will come out on the right-hand side.

On the end of the selector barrel is the cam pin set plate. Remove its bolt, and then take off the nuts holding the cam guide plate, set over the drum, on top of the crankcase. These nuts have locking tab washers, which will need to be flattened before they can be turned.

**Splitting the Crankcase.** Eight cross-headed screws hold the crankcase halves together—four 6 × 35 screws; two 6 × 55 screws; and one each of 6 × 45 and 6 × 65. Note carefully where each comes from, so that you will be able to replace it when the time for reassembly comes.

When all the screws are out, tap around the crankcase joint with a hardwood block or a rubber mallet. When the joint breaks, draw the left half of the crankcase upwards, off the right half, leaving the working parts in position in the right half of the case.

As the halves separate, the spacers of the rubber engine mounting will slip out. Do not lose them. The crankcase dowels may also come undone, as may the small spacer from the left-hand oil seal. Detach the crankcase gasket and discard it. A new one *must* be used on reassembly.

You can now proceed with the removal of the mechanical components. Draw out the kickstarter spindle and its associated parts. These are the pinion, pawl, spring/plunger, and thrust washers. There may also be a shim set between the thrust washer and the pinion boss. If so, it has been put there for adjustment and must not be omitted on rebuilding the unit.

Hardened screws passing through their sleeves hold the selector forks.. These screws engage in the cam groove running round the selector drum barrel. Their tab washers must be flattened, and a 10-mm box spanner then used to remove them. Then the cam guide and the selector drum can be detached. That done, drive out the mainshaft and remove the gear cluster, complete with selector forks. The pinions can be lifted off their shafts, but take care not to misplace the thrust washers which are used in these assemblies. They *must* go back in their correct positions. Note, too, that there is a circlip on each shaft—on the countershaft, between the second and third gear pinions; and on the mainshaft second and third gears.

**Crankshaft Removal.** Drive the crankshaft out of the right-hand crankcase, and test the big end bearing for wear by setting it at T.D.C. and

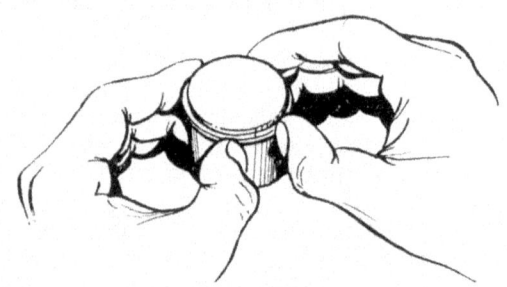

FIG. 37. REMOVING THE PISTON RINGS
Ease the piston rings out of their grooves by expanding them with the thumbs, as shown here.

pressing the con-rod up and down. There should be no perceptible play. If the bearing is worn an exchange crankshaft should be fitted.

**Bearing Removal.** The crankshaft is carried on three ball bearings—one on the drive side; two on the generator side. Oil seals are used on both sides of the crankcase. The counter shaft carrying the final drive sprocket runs in a ball bearing on the left and in a blind bush on the right; the main shaft in a bush on the left and in a ball bearing—held by a retainer plate secured by three countersunk screws—on the right. The kickstarter shaft has an oil seal on the right-hand case and the countershaft an oil seal on the left-hand case. In each instance, the oil seals must be removed before the bearings can be driven out, and in the case of the mainshaft bearing the main retainer plate must come off first.

The inner main bearing on the right-hand side has a thrust washer interposed between itself and the crank disc, and a spacer is set between the inner and outer bearings on that side.

**Bearing Insertion.** Before new bearings can be fitted, the case must be heated to 80°C (176°F). The new bearings will then slip home easily. Use new oil seals whenever new bearings are fitted.

**Piston Removal.** Remove the two circlips holding the gudgeon-pin, and heat the piston by wrapping round it a rag wrung out in hot water. When

# RENOVATING THE 50 C.C. MOTOR-CYCLE ENGINES 51

it has expanded sufficiently the gudgeon-pin can be pressed out of the piston and the assembly removed from the connecting rod.

**Piston Ring Removal.** The piston rings are simply eased out of their grooves with the thumbs. Take care not to snap them when doing this—

FIG. 38. PISTON RING POSITION

Each piston ring is stamped, as indicated, to show which is its upper face.

they are made of cast iron and are consequently very brittle. They should be expanded only enough to clear the edges of the groove (*see* Figs. 37, 38 and 39).

**Reassembly.** Generally speaking, reassembly is merely a reversal of the stripping technique set out here, and should present no difficulties. There is, however, one point on the clutch to be borne in mind. When fitting the plate which carries the spring studs, make sure that the mark "*S*,"

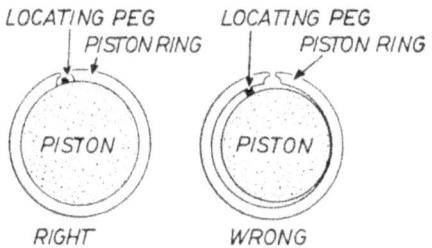

FIG. 39. PISTON RING LOCATION

If the rings were free to rotate, their ends would catch in the ports. To prevent this, the grooves have pegs. When refitting the rings make sure they engage properly and do not ride over the pegs.

one of the slots in the clutch body, one of the studs on the plate and the locating peg on the clutch centre face are aligned. Then, when fitting the plain steel plates—which, of course, alternate with the friction-faced plates—ensure that the dot is to the left of the stud which is in line with the peg. If this is not done you will not obtain the correct registration for the spring cups. Note, too, that the clutch should be refitted before —not after—the engine drive pinion.

When refitting the piston, make sure that the arrow on the crown is pointing forward, and that the chromium-plated ring is at the top.

# 7 Overhauling the Suzy engine

BASICALLY similar in layout to the engines used on the M 15 and M 15 D motor-cycles, the M 30 Suzy "mokick" engine is equally simple to work upon, the main difference being in the use of a centrifugally-controlled clutch in place of the manually-operated clutches of the motor-cycles.

**Preparatory Work.** This is done in the same way as described in Chapter Six, with the proviso that the legshields should be detached before, and not after cleaning commences. The shield is held, on each side, by two cross-headed screws and by a single bolt with large load-spreading washers. It comes away after these have been released and the protective mouldings detached.

**What Must Come Off?** Jobs for which it is essential that the engine unit should be removed from the frame are—

Work on the crankshaft; work on the mainshaft or secondary shaft of the gearbox; inspecting the selector cam and selector forks; renewing the kickstarter spindle, pawl, pawl spring, starter pinion or pawl roller; attention to bearings and bushes.

Virtually all other engine work can be carried out without removing the motor, but it is often convenient to lift the engine for work on the bench. The various operations are set out here as for a full engine strip. Where the work to be done does not necessitate removing the engine the relevant sections can be taken in isolation instead of being followed in sequence.

**Engine Removal.** Remove the induction stub bolts with a 10-mm open-ended spanner and free the pipe from the cylinder (*see* Fig. 40). Then remove the bolt securing the gear lever and ease it off its splines. With a cross-headed screwdriver, release the three screws which secure the left-hand crankcase cover and pull the cover from the unit. If it sticks, jar the joint with a block of hardwood.

You now have access to the drive chain. Turn the rear wheel until the spring connector link is accessible, and lever off the spring clip. Remove the link to break the chain, wiring the upper run to any convenient point on the machine and allowing the lower one to hang down.

Undo the knurled knob and take off the toolbox lid. Inside the frame and reached through an aperture normally covered by the lid is the snap connector cluster for the wiring. Undo this, and detach the sparking plug cap. Then release the two nuts holding the exhaust pipe to the flange on the cylinder, and pull the pipe clear. Do not disturb the clamp on the pipe adjacent to the rubber junction with the silencer. This is intended as a tensioner.

Place a heavy wooden box under the engine, so that it is well supported, and remove the nuts from the three engine mounting bolts. Take out the two bottom bolts, and then brace the engine with one hand while the top bolt is slid out. The engine is now free from the machine and can be pulled out and lifted on to the workbench.

Where a complete strip is envisaged, it is better to drain the oil while the unit is still in the frame. This is done by removing the oil filler plug

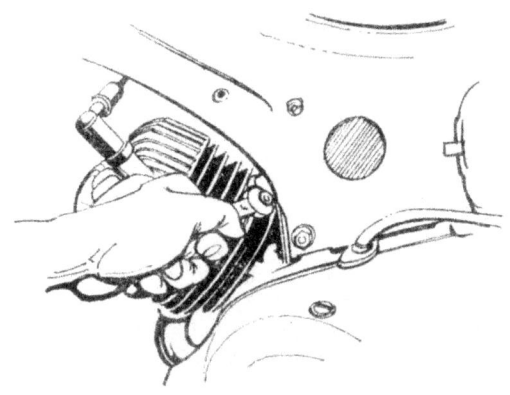

FIG. 40. INLET STUB MOUNTING NUTS

When removing the engine from the M 30, undo the nuts holding the inlet stub to the cylinder, and leave the stub in the frame when the engine is dropped out.

on top of the unit, on the right-hand side, and detaching the drain plug from the bottom of the unit, between the footrest attachment and the silencer. When all the oil has drained into the tray placed beneath the unit, loosely refit both plugs.

**Cylinder Head Removal.** Using the plug spanner supplied in the tool kit, detach the sparking plug. Then—working diagonally from side to side—remove the four head nuts. A 10-mm box spanner or socket is required here. The head can then be lifted from the studs. If it is tight, do not try to lever it up. Instead, jar it with a block of wood until the head joint parts.

**Cylinder Removal.** Turn the engine until the piston is at B.D.C. Then lift the barrel off its studs. Try not to tear the base gasket, which may tend to stick to the barrel on one side and the crankcase on the other. If it does tear a new one will have to be used on reassembly, but otherwise the old one may be refitted.

As the piston comes clear of the mouth of the barrel, support it so that it does not fall forward and get damaged.

**Flywheel Removal.** With the barrel off the engine, place hardwood blocks under the piston skirt and bring it down to trap them against the crankcase mouth. The crankshaft is now locked. Place a 14-mm box or socket spanner on the flywheel nut and undo it. Then screw in the special flywheel puller (Tool No. T 032) and draw the flywheel off the shaft. Do not misplace or damage the Woodruff key which locates it.

**Stator Removal.** Scribe a mark across the stator and on to the crankcase so that the correct timing can be reset without difficulty. Then remove the three cross-headed screws holding the stator plate, detach the lead from the neutral indicator switch, and slide the harness grommet out of position on the casing. The stator can now be detached. Place it inside the flywheel for safety.

**Neutral Indicator Switch.** This is held by three cross-headed screws. Under the switch is a contact spring, secured by a single cross-headed screw.

**Final Drive Sprocket.** Before the 26-mm nut holding the sprocket can be undone, the tab locking washer has to be flattened, using a hammer and drift. A special tool (No. T 027) is normally employed to hold the sprocket still while the nut is unscrewed, but it is possible to lock it satisfactorily by using a length of transmission chain. Under the sprocket —which is splined to the shaft—is a spacer. This should not be mislaid.

**Kickstarter Removal.** A single 10-mm bolt secures the kickstarter to its spindle. Undo this, and slide the starter pedal sideways to free it.

**Right-hand Crankcase Cover Removal.** Eight cross-headed screws secure this cover. Remove them, and pull off the cover and its gasket. Do not attempt to lever the cover off if the joint is stiff. Jar all round it with a block of hardwood until the joint frees. Attempts to force it off will result in a cracked casing.

**Clutch Removal.** Using a hammer and a suitable drift, flatten out the tab locking washer. Now insert the three pins of the special clutch-holding tool No. T 084 (it is essential to have this) into the holes on the clutch face, and hold the unit steady while the centre nut is removed by use of a 23-mm box spanner. Then take off the clutch sleeve hub retainer.

The clutch springs must now be compressed (preferably by using Tool No. T 085) until the clutch outer plate circlip can be eased down and out of its groove in the clutch body, so freeing the plates. The clutch housing can then be lifted away.

Normally, there will be no need for further dismantling, but if the clutch inner plate return springs are removed—they can be hooked out with long-nosed pliers—the inner plate, 18 steel balls, and the ball guide ring can all be lifted out.

# OVERHAULING THE SUZY ENGINE

**Primary Drive Pinion Removal.** Again blocking up between the piston skirt and the crankcase mouth, fix special tool No. T 083 on the driving pinion and use a 17-mm socket spanner to undo the pinion nut. Then drive the tool anti-clockwise with a hammer until the pinion is freed from its taper.

**Gearchange Mechanism Removal.** Remove the gearchange cam-stopper spring and release the 10-mm bolt with a socket or box spanner. The cam stopper and washer can then be removed. Next, detach the two bolts (10-mm) holding the gear selector cam guide. On the left-hand side of the machine, release the circlip on the gearchange spindle, and remove the washer. The shaft and return spring will then pull out as a unit from the right-hand case.

**Piston Removal.** Remove the circlips which locate the gudgeon pin in the piston boss. Then, with a rag wrung out in hot water, expand the piston until the pin can be pressed out sufficiently to clear the small end.

**Piston Ring Removal.** Spring the two piston rings out of their grooves by expanding them with the thumbs. Be careful not to overdo this—they are made of cast iron and are thus very brittle.

**Splitting the Crankcase.** Having reached this stage, loosen the two screws which hold the engine sprocket back cover to the crankcase, and detach the cover. Then remove the eight other screws holding the cases together, the three screws of the transmission section coming out first. Do not overlook the very rearmost screw, which is normally hidden under the sprocket back cover.

The crankcase is now placed left-side upwards and the joint between the two halves is broken with blows from a rubber mallet or a block of wood. Lift off the left-hand case, taking great care that the gears, shafts, etc., stay in the right-hand case. If the gearshafts are lifted with the left-hand case, 18 bearing balls will suddenly fall out and may be lost or damaged.

This is probably as far as the average owner would wish to go. It permits the fitting of a replacement crankchaft and, with care, of main bearings. The mainshaft bearing in the left-hand case can also be renewed. For the method of renewing bearings, refer to page 50.

**Rebuilding the Unit.** Generally speaking, reassembly is nothing more nor less than stripping in reverse, and no undue difficulties should be encountered. Note, however, that when refitting the primary drive pinion the nut must be tightened to 250–400 kg/cm (20–36 lb/ft). If the gear-selector-shaft return spring has been taken off, push the pawl so that it does not contact the selector cam, and insert the shaft. Fit the pawl to the slot inside the cam and, after installing the shaft, refit the washer and circlip on the left-hand case.

**Clutch Reassembly.** There are five ordinary clutch friction plates and one clutch inner friction plate. At first glance this is very similar to the others, but it is thicker and has a 1-mm slot cut on one of its teeth. When you get to the stage of refitting these plates to the clutch, do not mix them up: the inner plate goes in first, followed by a steel plate; then the five friction plates, alternated with plain plates, are fitted.

Clutch assembly begins by fitting the housing collar to the shaft. Next, the ball guide ring and the 18 steel balls are set in the clutch housing, and the spring holes are aligned. The inner plate return springs are then fitted with the help of long-nosed pliers, which are used to pull them on to the inner plate.

The clutch housing is offered up to the unit and the clutch sleeve hub spacer and hub are added. The clutch sleeve hub holes are on the outside. Next, the plates are put in—as already detailed—followed by the outer cork plate, the clutch springs and the clutch outer plate. The circlip is then refitted after the whole assembly has been compressed. Then, the lock washer and the hub nut are added, the nut first being taken up finger tight and then securely tightened down with the help of special tool T 084. Finally, the lock washer is turned over one of the flats to lock it.

**Neutral Indicator Switch Lead.** It is important not to trap the indicator switch lead between the crankcase and the left-hand crankcase cover when the unit is being reassembled. This is normally the cause of the trouble if the neutral indicator light remains on when the gears are engaged.

**Retiming the Engine.** Retiming should not be necessary unless the contact-breaker mechanism has been renewed. Simply set the stator plate to its original position—as shown by your scribed marks. Where retiming is thought desirable, follow the instructions given in Chapter Five.

**Filling with Oil.** When the unit has been re-installed in the machine, fully tighten the drain plug and again remove the filler plug. Then pour in 1·2 Imperial pints (1·4 U.S. pints) of grade 20/40 S.A.E. motor oil of your usual brand. In hot climates, a 30/40 grade may be used. You can ascertain that the oil level is correct by removing the level screw which is set just ahead of the kickstarter, low down on the right-hand side of the machine. When oil starts to come out of the hole, with the machine level, the transmission casing contains sufficient.

# 8 Overhauling the 80 c.c. engine

In general design, the 80 c.c. power unit of the K 10 and K 11 motorcycles is similar to the 50 c.c. motor, and the method of stripping and rebuilding is in fact much the same. Therefore, the preceding chapters should also be read.

**Engine Removal.** If a front shield has been fitted, remove its securing bolts with a 12-mm spanner. Turn off the fuel, and carry out the cleaning operation described previously.

Remove the carburettor cover (a 10-mm spanner and a cross-headed screwdriver are needed here) and detach the fuel pipe (10-mm spanner), the starter control cable (14-mm spanner), the throttle slide, and the air cleaner hose (cross-headed screwdriver).

With a 10-mm spanner, take out the securing bolt of the gearchange pedal and slide the pedal off its spindle. Then remove the left-hand crankcase cover, which is held by five cross-headed screws. Bring the chain connecting link on to the sprocket and remove it, wiring the top run of the chain to any convenient point and allowing the bottom run to hang loose.

All that work was on the left-hand side. Now go to the right-hand side and remove the exhaust pipe. This is held to its flange by a screwed ring, which is normally undone by use of a pin spanner (Tool No. T 082). With care, however, it may be turned off by tapping with a soft-metal drift and hammer, with the other side of the exhaust stub supported by the hand.

Now drain the transmission oil, remove the silencer, the kickstarter, and the cover of the air cleaner. Detach the element—it is held by two cross-headed screws—and ease the wiring harness snap connector cluster out of the frame. Disconnect the black, yellow, blue and red/green leads. Now place a stout wooden box under the engine to support it, and undo the nuts of the three engine mounting bolts and the two bolts on the front down tube. All are of 14-mm size. Withdraw the bottom bolts first, then the top ones, and the engine is free.

**Carburettor Removal.** Loosen the screw on the carburettor clamp, and gently slide the instrument rearwards to disengage it from its stub. If it is stiff, twist it from side to side a little as you do so.

**Cylinder Head Removal.** Four 10-mm set bolts hold the cylinder head to the barrel. Remove these, working diagonally from one to another,

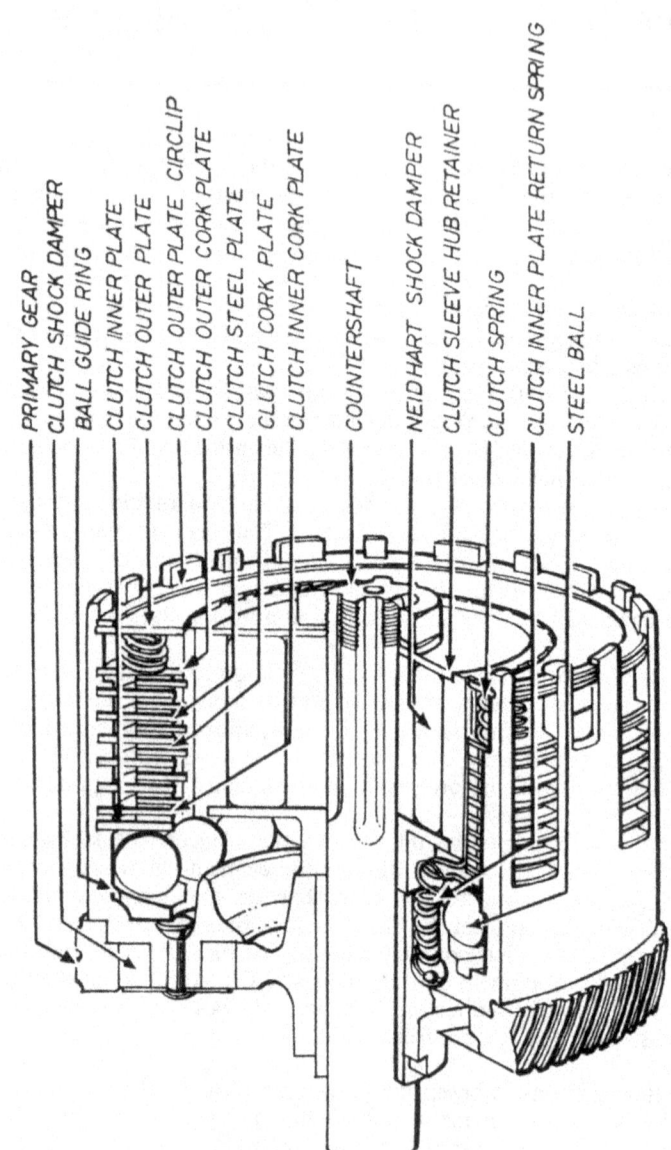

Fig. 41. The Suzuki Automatic Clutch in Cross-Section
The relationship of the various parts of the automatic clutch is shown clearly here.

and the head and gasket can be lifted off. If the head sticks, jar it with a block of softwood.

**Cylinder Barrel Removal.** The barrel is held to the crankcase by four nuts on its flange. Each has a spring washer. Remove the nuts—again, working from side to side on a diagonal—having first set the piston to B.D.C. Then lift the barrel, taking care to support the piston as it emerges from the mouth of the cylinder.

**Flywheel Magneto Removal.** Insert hardwood blocks under the piston skirt so that the crank assembly is locked against the crankcase, and undo the centre nut (14-mm box spanner or socket) on the magneto. Take out the flat and spring washers beneath it, and screw in the flywheel extractor (Tool No. T 032). Draw off the flywheel. Scribe a mark from the stator plate to the crankcase so that the timing can be accurately reset, and remove the three screws and washers on the periphery of the plate. Take out the screw holding the neutral indicator switch lead. The stator car then be eased off, and placed in the flywheel for safe keeping.

**Detaching the Drive Sprocket.** Engage a gear, block the piston skirt, and use a drift to flatten the locking tab washer on the sprocket nut. Then fit a 26-mm box spanner with a stout tommy bar on to the nut, and jar the bar with a hammer until the nut frees. The sprocket and its distance piece can then be slipped off the shaft.

**Detaching the Clutch Cover.** On the right-hand side of the engine, the clutch cover is held by eight cross-headed screws. Remove all of them, and if necessary jar the joint with a softwood block.

**Stripping the Clutch.** The clutch of the 80 c.c. Suzuki is of unusual but simple design, in that the springs are held by means of dimples and pins instead of the more usual studs and nuts (*see* Figs. 41, 42, 43, 44 and 45).

A special tool (a clutch spring hook—T 042) is needed for the first operation. One of these could be improvised from a cycle spoke bent to form a small hook at one end, and looped several times round a tommy bar at the other. The hook is inserted into the eye of each spring and the spring is pulled slightly upwards to take the pressure off the lateral pin. The pin is then pulled out, and the spring tension released. There are six pins to be removed in all. When they are all out, lift off the pressure plate. Then take out the four drive plates and the four driven plates, the release rod, and the push rod.

With a drift, flatten the tab washer on the clutch centre nut. Engage a gear, block the piston, and with a 26-mm box spanner undo the nut. The clutch hub and body can then be removed from the shaft, followed by the body collar and the thrust washer.

The springs are held in the clutch body by their lower coil being looped

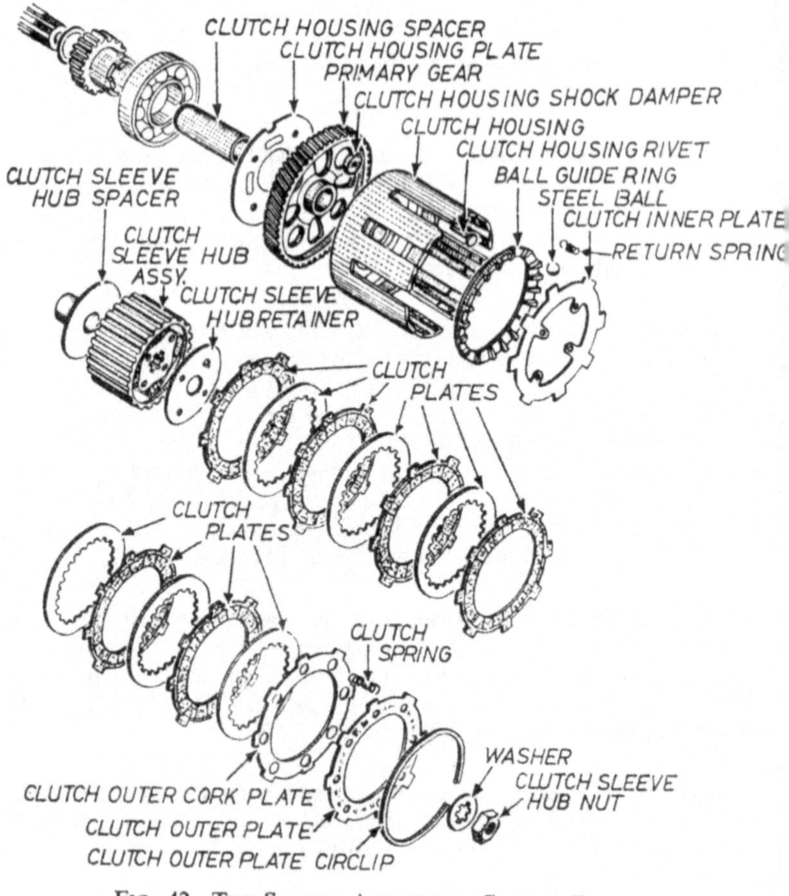

FIG. 42. THE SUZUKI AUTOMATIC CLUTCH EXPLODED

This type of clutch is used only on the M 30 Suzy scooterette. Its action is controlled by balls operated by centrifugal force.

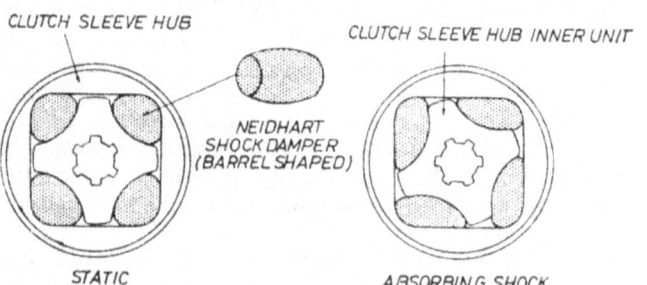

FIG. 43. THE CLUTCH-CENTRE SHOCK ABSORBER

Jerkiness in the transmission is prevented by this "cush-drive" unit built into the clutch. The rubber inserts deform under sudden load to cushion "snatch."

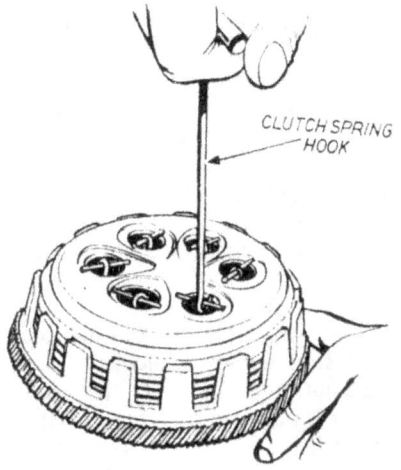

FIG. 44. CLUTCH SPRING PIN REMOVAL

The clutch spring securing pins on the 80 c.c. model are removed by inserting a special hook into the spring loop, and lifting sufficiently to free the pin from spring tension. It is then slipped out. A suitable hook can be made from a bicycle spoke.

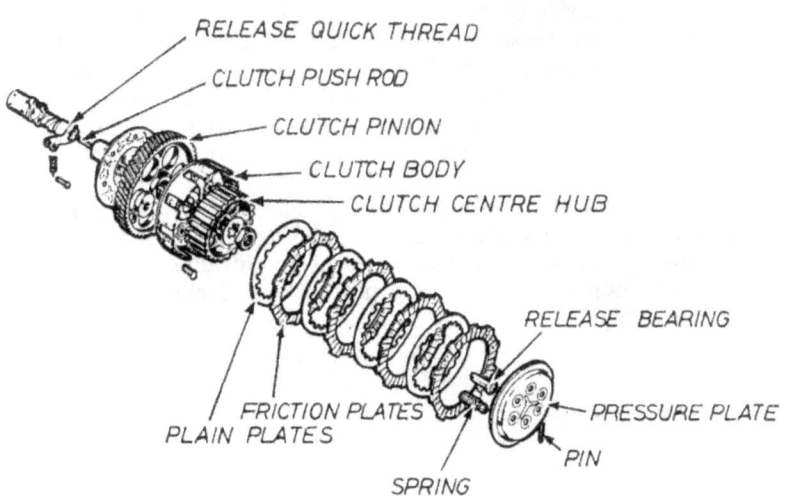

FIG. 45. THE K 10/K 11 CLUTCH

This "exploded" drawing shows the strong but simple construction of the 80 c.c. clutch, an unusual feature of which is the spring fixing by means of pegs. The 50 c.c. motor-cycles have a similar unit, but with the springs retained by studs and nuts.

into dimples formed in the body face. Removal is simple—just disengage the spring by twisting it.

**Removing the Selector Mechanism.** With a screwdriver, prise off the circlip from the selector shaft. This shaft can then be lifted out complete.

**Kickstarter Return Spring Removal.** Detach the return-spring guide and, with a pair of pliers, grasp the end of the spring to pull it away. Take off the circlip which is located behind the spring, and pull off the spring holder.

**Freeing the Primary-drive Pinion.** Flatten the locking tab washer with a drift, and lock the piston skirt with blocks of hardwood. Fit a 21-mm spanner on the centre nut, and free it. If necessary, jar the spanner with a hammer. The pinion is not held by a taper, but is located on the shaft by a Woodruff key. If it is stiff, insert a pair of tyre levers under it and ease it off its shaft. Remove the key and put it in a place of safety. Being small, it can easily be lost.

**Neutral Indicator Switch Removal.** Detach the three cross-headed screws which hold the switch, and take out the switch body and its gasket.

**Separating the Crankcase Halves.** Remove the chaincase extension from the left-hand side of the unit—it is held by two cross-headed screws—and then free off the seven 6-mm cross-headed screws which hold the crankcase halves together. Jar the joint with a block of softwood until it parts. Set the unit on the bench with the right-hand side downwards, and lift off the left-hand crankcase, leaving the crankshaft and transmission in the right-hand case. The rubber-asbestos gasket should come away with the left-hand case.

Crankshaft, piston and bearing removal, etc., can now be carried out as already described for the 50 c.c. engines. Rebuilding is a reversal of the stripping procedure, and should present no difficulties. However, the normal workshop practice of using new gaskets, locking washers, etc., should be followed.

# 9 The cycle parts

APART from the periodic checking and greasing of the head bearings and lubricating the front and rear wheel bearings, maintenance on the cycle side is confined to routine adjustments to the brakes and drive chain. Overhauls are sparse, too. As the brake linings wear out the efficiency of the "anchors" must be restored by fitting shoes with new friction surfaces; faulty bearings must be replaced by new ones; and the drive chain and the sprockets will require renewal once the machine has done a really considerable mileage.

That—apart from pumping up the tyres—is the sum total. But you cannot afford to neglect this side of the work, because much of the pleasure of riding—and virtually all the safety—depends upon the condition of the frame, forks, wheels, tyres and brakes. The same care must be lavished on them as is so frequently given to the more "romantic" engine.

**Steering Head Bearings.** The steering head is the last refuge of the now-unfashionable adjustable type of bearing. The lower race consists of two split bearing tracks in which run 22 steel bearing balls. The upper race is of similar construction, except that its top half is threaded to the stem of the forks. By screwing it up and down the play in the bearings can be increased or decreased.

**Adjusting the Head Bearings.** Raise the machine, by blocking under the crankcase, until the front wheel is clear of the ground. Then place the first finger of your left hand on the joint between the two halves of the lower race and grasp the top of the forks with the other hand. Try to rock the forks by twisting back and forth along the centre-line of the machine. If you can feel the lower race moving backwards and forwards as you do this the bearings need adjustment. An alternative method is to sit on the machine with the front brake applied, place your hand on the top race, and rock the whole 'bike backwards and forwards. Tell-tale movement or a clicking sound shows the need for adjustment.

The adjuster lies below the top bridge of the fork (*see* Fig. 46), which will have to be detached. To do so, take off the handlebars (jt may be necessary to free the indicator lamp wires on some models) and let them hang over the headlamp. Then flatten the tab locking washer on the stem bolt, and undo the bolt itself. On telescopic-fork models undo the two fork plug bolts. The bridge can then be taken off.

Next, the locking ring must be freed. There is a special tool for this (No. T 028) but in its absence you can turn off the ring with a hammer and a soft-metal drift. Do *not* use a steel drift, or you will damage the ring. The knurled upper race is now free to be moved. Simply turn it in by hand as far as it will go, using light hand pressure. Then test for play again. If there is still noticeable play, screw the race in more firmly. If the play cannot be removed by this means the bearings will require renewal. Normally, however, you will find that the slack is quickly taken up. When you reach this point, back off the ring by a quarter-turn. Then

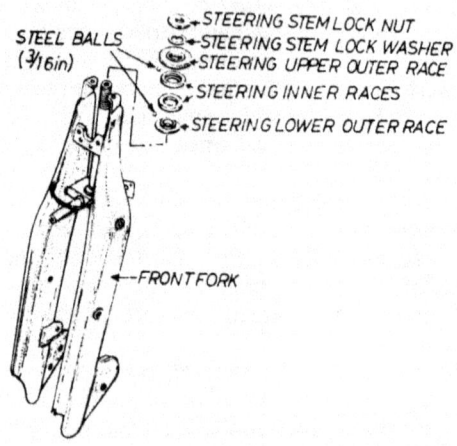

Fig. 46. The Suzuki Front Fork

This illustration shows the construction of the main fork blade and the nature of the steering head bearings. The upper bearing has an adjustable outer race which enables play in the head to be taken up.

re-check the play and, if all is in order, screw down the locking ring to hold the new adjustment.

Refit the fork bridge and the stem bolt, using a new locking washer, and refit the plugs on telescopic-fork models. Refit the handlebars, and the job is done.

Don't, however, substitute one fault for another by over-tightening the head bearings. The front forks must be free to turn, otherwise the machine will not steer properly. The best check here is to knock the forks from side to side. They should flip over quite freely from one lock to the other. If there is any stiffness, or any tendency to stick in one position in their travel, then the adjustment is too tight and the knurled ring must be slackened by a fraction of a turn at a time until absolutely free fork movement is again obtained. As soon as you have this setting, check the play in the head. If it is excessive you have faulty bearings and, again, renewal is necessary.

**Bearing Renewal.** To renew the bearings one must remove the front forks from the machine. This is done by freeing the speedometer cable and the various snap connectors inside the headlamp cowling, and then taking off the front wheel. The steering head bridge is next removed, as just described, and the locking ring is undone. Then the knurled upper race is screwed off the stem, and the bearing balls are lifted out of the race. The forks must be supported all the time by one hand under the lower bridge.

Now, the forks are lowered carefully, and the lower race bearing balls

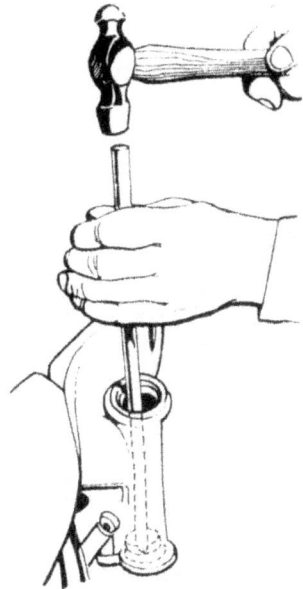

FIG. 47. DRIVING OUT STEERING HEAD RACES
When the tracks of the races in the steering head need renewal, the old ones are driven out by inserting a long punch and striking sharply with a hammer.

should come away with them. Let the forks drop until the stem is clear of the head, and lift them away from the machine.

If the bearing is to be renewed completely, take out and discard all the balls. On the other hand, where the object is simply to clean and regrease the bearings, the balls from each race must be collected and placed separately, ready for cleaning and re-installation. In such a case, there is no need to remove the tracks from the fork or head. They are simply cleaned in place, their condition checked, and the fresh lubricant applied before rebuilding is commenced.

The races should have tracks which are completely free from pitting or surface damage. If there is any sign of a blemish on the surface of a track it must be renewed—otherwise, it will soon break up completely and the whole job will have to be done again. The same applies to the bearing balls. When these—like the tracks—have been well washed in petrol and dried they should be examined. If any are rusted or pitted, fit new races. Don't try to use new bearing balls on old tracks or vice versa. The older surfaces will ruin the new ones in no time.

Where complete renewal is planned, use a long steel drift, inserted from the opposite end of the steering head, to drive the tracks out (*see* Fig. 47). Then use a hammer and cold chisel to cut the fixed lower track away from the steering stem (*see* Fig. 48). New tracks are driven into place with the aid of a block of softwood interposed between the track and the hammer head. Make sure they enter squarely and are properly seated.

To refit the forks, first thoroughly grease the tracks. Then fit the 22

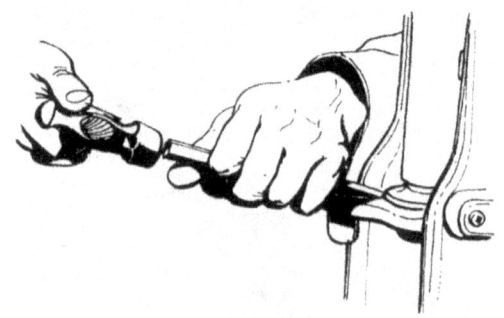

FIG. 48. CUTTING AWAY THE LOWER FORK RACE
To remove the old race from the fork stem, it is necessary to cut through it with a cold chisel, used as shown.

balls into both upper and lower races, pressing them well into the grease, having first given each ball its own coating of grease so that it will not make dry contact anywhere. Press the balls into the grease in the lower race, and it will hold them in position while the fork is being offered up. Note, too, that although 22 balls may seem to give a loose fit, and leave room for one more, this is intentional. The vital working clearance must not be taken up by inserting an extra ball.

With the fork stem in place through the steering head, screw on the new upper track and bring the head bearing into adjustment as previously described. With old bearings which have simply been re-lubricated—a job which needs to be done only at intervals of 10,000 miles—there is no need to disturb the setting after it has been made. New bearings, however, may settle down; and it is advisable to test the adjustment again after 1,000 miles have been covered.

**Removing Front Fork Spring Units.** On the swinging-link Suzuki fork it is a simple matter to remove the spring units for renewal or inspection (*see* Fig. 49). First, take off the front wheel. Fit a 17-mm spanner on to the swinging-link pivot bolt, and with a 14-mm spanner undo the nut on the inner face of the fork leg.

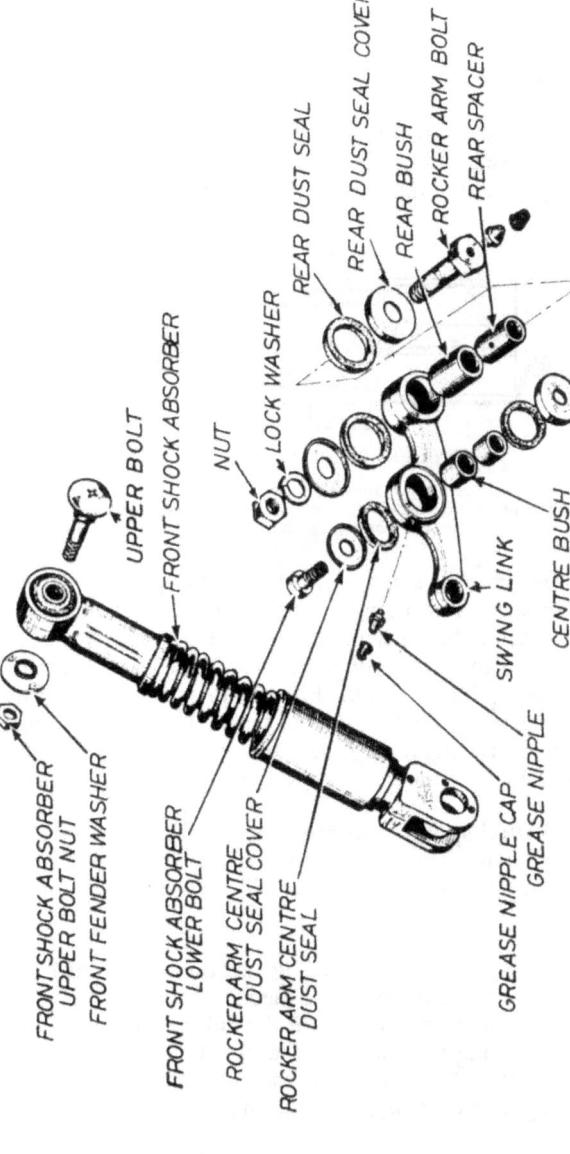

Fig. 49. Swinging-Link Front Springing

This shows how far the front springing can be stripped during overhaul. The spring/damper unit must be renewed if it is faulty, since it cannot be serviced.

Next, take off the 12-mm nuts holding the mudguard, and with a cross-headed screwdriver undo the set screw which holds the top mounting of the spring unit. The unit, complete with swinging link, can then be drawn down the fork leg.

To detach the link, hold the fixing nut with a 12-mm spanner and use a cross-headed screwdriver to undo the pivot screw.

**Renewing Fork Bushes.** In time, the bushes in the fork links tend to wear. They can be removed and replaced quite simply, since they are merely a press fit. You can make up a simple tool (*see* Fig. 50) for this.

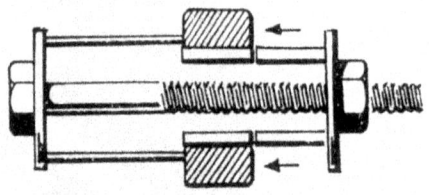

FIG. 50. BUSH RENEWAL

A simple tool you can make yourself from a nut and bolt, a spacer, and a couple of washers which can be used for renewing bushes. Its use is described on this page.

Obtain a bolt three times the length of the bush, and a nut to fit. You will need two large washers and a spacer with an internal diameter slightly greater than the outside diameter of the bush. Place one washer on top of this spacer and pass the bolt through it. Lead the bolt through the bush and butt the spacer against the link. Fit the new bush on the other end of the bolt, aligning it carefully with the old bush. Then add the remaining washer and the nut. By tightening the nut down on to the washer, the new bush can be used to drive out the old one.

**Spring Units.** Suzuki spring units are sealed and cannot, therefore, be stripped for renovation. The only possible course, where the unit has weakened, has been damaged, or is losing oil, is to replace it with a new component.

**Reassembling the Spring Units.** Having thoroughly cleaned all components, reassemble in the following sequence. First, lubricate the felt dust seals on the links with engine oil. Fit the link to the spring unit, with the nut of the lower fitting so positioned that it will lie on the inside of the leg. Offer up the unit to the fork, insert the swinging link pivot pin, and then bolt the spring unit to its upper mounting.

**Wheel Removal, All Models.** On swinging-link models, take out the brake torque arm bolt at each end of the arm. Then detach the spindle nut—having first freed its split pin—and draw out the spindle. If it is tight, revolving it as you pull will loosen it. The wheel, complete with brake, can then be dropped out. Pull the brake out of the drum, leaving the cables attached unless you wish to work on the back-plate itself. In

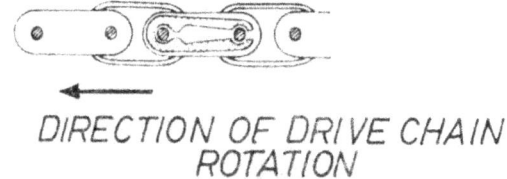

FIG. 51. FITTING THE SPRING LINK

It is essential that when the spring link is fitted to the chain, the closed end should face towards the direction of rotation. Otherwise, the chain may come open.

that case, free the brake cable in the normal way, and take out the speedo drive cable. On the M 12, K 10 and K 11 models, this is held by a circlip. On all other models it is secured by a collared sleeve.

There is also a steel distance-piece set in the grease seal on the plain side of the hub. Be very careful not to lose this when taking the wheel out.

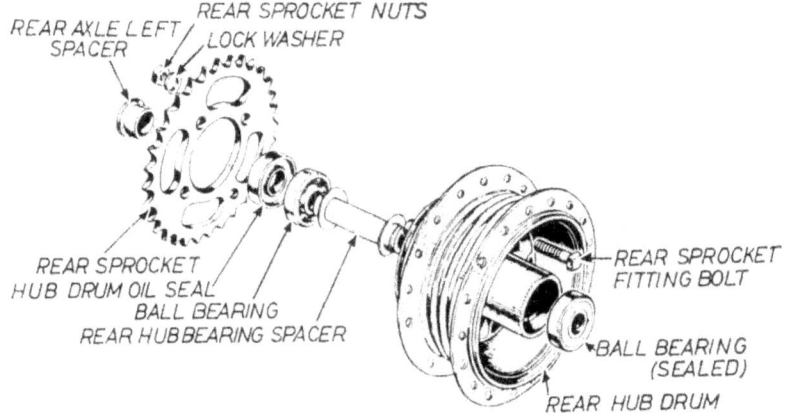

FIG. 52. THE REAR HUB

Ball bearings are shrunk into the hub casing, and are pre-packed with lubricating grease.

**Rear Wheel Removal, All Models.** Where a chaincase is fitted, detach its rear end and turn the wheel until the connecting link can be reached. Split the chain by removing this link, securing each end to the machine with a loop of wire or string so that it does not fall into the case.

Next, slacken the nut holding the brake torque arm to the suspension member, and then remove the nut which secures the arm on the brake

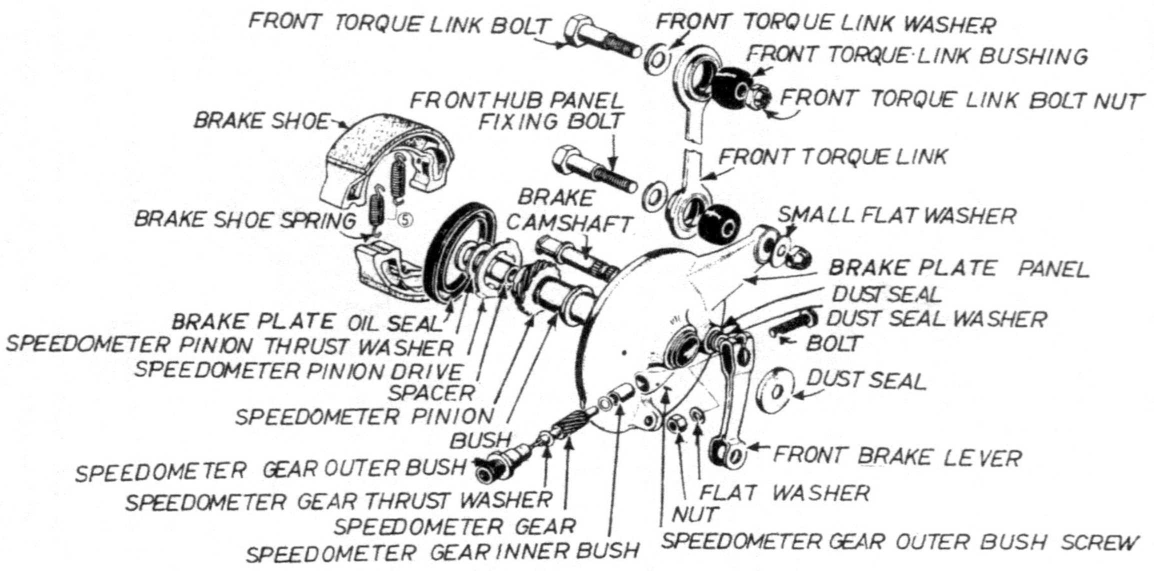

FIG. 53. THE SUZUKI FRONT BRAKE

How the front brake of the Suzuki machines is set out. Note the built-in drive for the speedometer incorporated in the back plate.

plate. Take off the spindle nut, withdraw the spindle, and drop out the wheel with the brake still attached. This can be done quite easily after removal of the distance pieces on both sides of the wheel, but note that these may be different and that their position should be recorded for your guidance on reassembly.

Detach the brake-operating arm, leaving it attached to the brake rod,

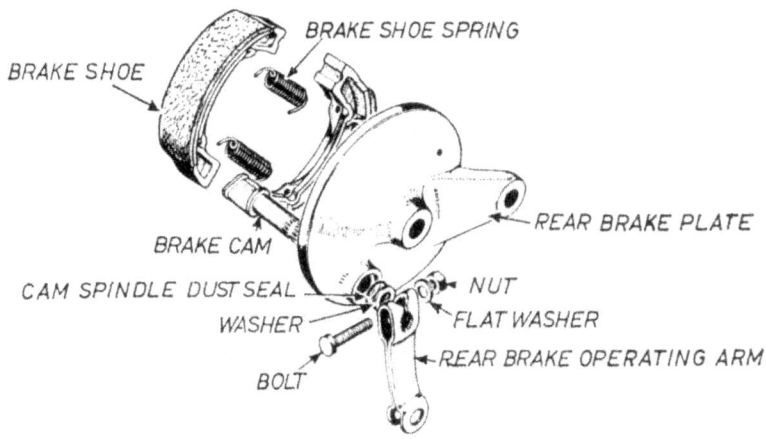

FIG. 54. THE SUZUKI REAR BRAKE
Thanks to the absence of the speedometer drive, the layout of the rear brake is simpler.

rather than undo the rod itself and so lose the brake adjustment. This should be necessary only if there is work to be done on the back-plate itself.

**Wheel Replacement, All Models.** Refitting a wheel is merely the reverse of its removal, and no difficulty should be experienced. Note, however, that when refitting the spring link to the chain the closed end of the clip must face in the chain's direction of travel—i.e. to the front (*see* Fig. 51).

**Wheel Bearing Renewal.** Unless the bearings are worn, there is no need to take them out of the hubs. Renewal is simple: a steel drift is inserted from the opposite side of the wheel and the bearing is driven out by two or three clean strokes of a hammer. The bearing on the brake side is a sealed type; that on the plain side a normal ball race. They are installed by driving-in with a hammer, with a softwood block interposed so that the bearing is not damaged in the process. The "exploded" drawings (*see* Figs. 52, 53 and 54) make the construction of the hubs quite clear.

**Brake Renovation.** All that need be done to renovate the brakes is to remove worn linings and fit new ones (*see* Fig. 55). This is best done by using replacement relined shoes. The old shoes are detached by pulling them outwards, together, against the tension of their springs so that they clear the pivots. Take off the springs, link them on to the new shoes—the coil of each spring goes uppermost—and pull the two shoes apart

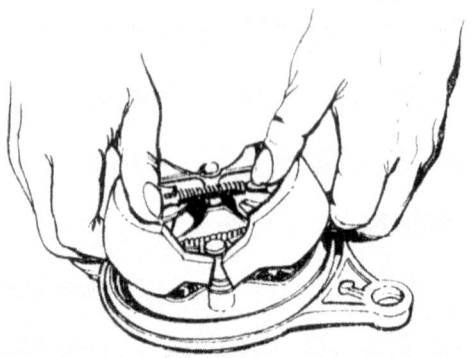

FIG. 55. DETACHING THE BRAKE SHOES

The brake shoes are held to the pivot and cam only by the pressure of the two pull-off springs. They are removed by pulling them outwards and then lifting to clear the cam and the pivot.

again so that they can be set on the lower pivot first, then on the operating cam.

Before reassembling the back-plate to the drum, wipe away all brake dust with a dry rag, and *very* lightly oil the springs and the cam pivot.

**Rear Sprocket Renewal.** After a long period of use, the teeth of the rear wheel sprocket may become hooked or badly worn. If so, you will have to replace not just the sprocket itself but also the engine sprocket and the chain. It is useless renewing just one part by itself. A new sprocket will soon be ruined by a worn chain, while sprockets which have had their day will play havoc with a new chain within a matter of a few miles.

To renew the rear wheel sprocket take off the wheel and remove the brake back-plate. Then undo the four 12-mm sprocket nuts, and tap the sprocket off the hub.

Fit the new sprocket, and re-tighten the nuts. When they have been securely fastened, complete the job by centre-punching the bolt and the nut so that they cannot move relative to each other.

# 10 Trouble tracing

When a doctor wishes to diagnose a patient's illness he works methodically, listing the various symptoms to build up an overall picture of the complaint. This, done, he can identify it and give treatment accordingly.

Exactly the same type of diagnosis has to be made if a motor-cycle engine refuses to work. Obviously, there is a fault—some reason why the engine will not work—and before any fault can be cured it must first be located and identified. The search for it must be just as methodical as is the doctor's approach.

If certain requirements are being fulfilled then the engine *must* work. If it is not working, then it follows that one—or more—of these requirements is not being met, and fault tracing boils down to discovering which it is, and why it is not being supplied.

An engine *must* work if the correct charge of fuel-air mixture is being induced into the crankcase, transferred to the cylinder, properly compressed, fired at the right moment, and the residue properly exhausted. Only an obvious mechanical failure could otherwise stop the unit from firing.

Consequently, fault tracing should always begin with an investigation into these five main requirements, and logically it would start with checking the petrol supply by peering into the tank to see that, in fact, there is a supply of fuel available. The next step should then be the equally obvious one of checking that the fuel is turned on and, if the tank level is low, that it is turned to the reserve position.

Once assured that the tank does contain fuel and that the tap is correctly set, the next check on the list is to ascertain whether or not the fuel is reaching the carburettor. It could be prevented by a blockage in the tap, by a blockage in the pipe, by an air lock, by a choked filter, or by a jammed needle valve.

Normally, this initial check will have taken only a minute or so to carry out, but it will have given one of two quite definite answers. Either fuel is reaching the carburettor, or it is not. If it is not, then you have found at least a contributory cause of the trouble, and this should be rectified before proceeding. If it is reaching the carburettor, you can pass on to the next stage which, with a two-stroke, must always be to check the sparking plug, especially if carburettor flooding has occurred.

Where an engine has been badly over-flooded, neat fuel will be trapped in the crankcase, and there will be no chance of starting. Take out the sparking plug, drain all fuel from the float chamber, and switch off the petroil. Then open the throttle wide, so that you admit as much air as possible, and turn the unit over on the kickstarter, briskly, about a dozen times. This should eject most of the trapped fuel. If the plug is wet, dry it. If necessary, burn the petrol off by holding the plug in the flame of a cigarette lighter or a match, using extreme care, and then replace it. Connect the H.T. lead, and operate the kickstarter. If the engine then fires, turn on the fuel. If it does not, turn on the fuel, allow a few seconds for the float chamber to fill, and then kick it again. It should then work satisfactorily.

If the initial inspection of the fuel system has brought no obvious fault to light, the next stage of the fault tracing should be switched to the ignition system. This is always a strong suspect with two-strokes, which tend to be very touchy indeed about their sparking plugs. So, first of all, remove the plug and examine the gap. Obviously this gap should be clear, but two-strokes can suffer from a condition called "whiskering." Under the influence of heat, metallic particles contained in the fuel tend to weld themselves to the plug electrodes, until they eventually bridge the gap completely. When this happens, of course, no spark occurs, since the high-tension current can follow the easier path to earth provided by the whisker joining the electrodes. A whisker is cleared simply by flicking it away with the blade of a pen-knife or with a feeler gauge. At a pinch, a piece of thin cardboard or a folded piece of paper will suffice. Then give the plug a clean with a wire brush and regap it before replacing it. Persistent whiskering is a sign that something else is wrong, too. It can indicate that the wrong grade of plug is fitted, or that the engine is running too hot. This, in turn, points to poor scavenging or a weak mixture, and should suggest that either the exhaust system is becoming choked or that a joint is leaking.

Where inspection of the plug shows the spark gap to be clear and neither over-wide nor too narrow, connect the plug to the H.T. lead and place its metal body in contact with the cylinder. Arrange matters so that you can easily see the gap while operating the kickstarter, and then turn the motor over smartly. A good fat spark should jump across the plug points. Repeat the check several times, and if no spark is obtained substitute a brand-new plug—an essential "spare" which should always be carried—and try again. If the new plug sparks and the old one didn't, the obvious inference is that the plug insulation has broken down, and fitting the new plug in its place should cure the trouble.

If no spark is obtained with the new plug, however, then the trouble lies somewhere between the sparking-plug terminal and the magneto, and a more exhaustive examination will have to be made.

Examine the H.T. lead minutely throughout its length, checking the terminals and inspecting the insulation for signs of cracks or perished areas which could be leading to a short-circuit. If you are doubtful about it, try the effect of substituting a spare length of H.T. lead and retesting with that. Examine all the electrical connexions on the H.T. and L.T. side of machines with an external coil.

Finally, remove the inspection plate and take a look at the contact-breaker points. Open them fully, and see if they are worn or dirty. Clean them by inserting a clean slip of card, close the points lightly on it, and withdraw it against their pressure. Do this two or three times, until the card comes away clean. Then open the points fully again and check the gap with a feeler gauge. If all is apparently in order you have then done all that is possible on the electrical side, so far as roadside checking is concerned. A full ignition test is a garage job.

Complete engine failure for any other cause is unlikely, save in the remote event of all the piston rings being broken following a seizure. Other troubles are more likely to show themselves in reduced performance or in erratic running.

One of the likelier causes of a lack of pulling power, for instance, is loss of compression, and it is possible, where this is suspected, to deduce where the fault lies from the way the engine behaves. If the crankcase seals have failed there will be a tendency for the unit to spit back through the carburettor, since extra air will be induced into the crankcase, thus weakening the mixture. Where the head joint is fractured, a characteristic hissing noise may be heard as gas is driven through the gap. In both cases the unit will tend to run hot and this, in turn, aggravates the trouble.

Following a seizure, as we have noted, the rings may have fractured. Or, on an engine which has not been decarbonized regularly, the rings may have "gummed up" in their grooves. This not only reduces both crankcase and cylinder compression, but it also allows oil to be driven from the case into the cylinder. This oil burns, and the resulting smoke issuing from the tail pipe is a good clue to watch for. If at any time you have partially seized your engine, and immediately afterwards it loses performance and begins to smoke, the only wise course is to stop immediately. The rings have almost certainly gone, and any further running could seriously damage the bore. This is especially the case where a ring has broken to form a sharp edge which will act as a highly efficient cutting tool. Then the engine can be ruined.

One puzzling fault is pre-ignition. The engine "pinks" continually— a metallic tinkling sound—and will even continue to run when the ignition is cut. This is caused by carbon deposits in the head becoming red hot and igniting the mixtures before the spark occurs. The cure is to decarbonize as soon as you possibly can.

Exactly the same process of elimination has to be followed when tracing faults in the lighting system. Faced with electricity, of course, most laymen simply give it best first time: but in fact electrical work is reasonably straightforward provided that magic word "circuit" is borne in mind. Circuits are the key to electricity. If electricity is present and the circuit is complete then the current *must* flow through it. If electricity is present but is not flowing then it follows that the circuit is not complete.

Faulty circuits are of two types: the open-circuit and the short-circuit. In the first case there is a complete break and the wires on the side of the breakage remote from the electrical source are "dead." In the case of a short-circuit the current is still flowing, but is following a shorter path to earth, as would happen, for instance, if one end of a live lead had become detached from its terminal and had earthed itself on the bodywork.

Obviously, then, the first stage is to find out which wire is affected, and to do this it is necessary to be able to read a wiring diagram. Such a diagram may at first sight appear disconcertingly like a plan of a railway marshalling yard, and oddly enough it is not at all a bad idea to think of it as such. The leads become railway lines, and the current the train which has to pass over them. Remember, though, that one important main line is not shown. This is the earth return, formed by the actual framework of the motor-cycle itself. All the components are connected to this earth, which, therefore, forms one complete half of the circuit.

When really complicated circuits are involved, it sometimes helps to trace them out individually, placing tracing paper over the wiring diagram and following the various lines until you have a picture of the complete circuit, with all its intermediate "stations" marked.

Having found the circuit, the next job is to check it. First, obviously, you have to discover whether any current is flowing or not, and here a test rig helps immensely. One can be made quite simply with a bulb, a bulb-holder, and a length of electrical lead. First, place the bulb-holder against one battery terminal, and then touch the other terminal with the end of the lead. The bulb should light. If not, it shows that the battery is flat, and it will have to be re-charged before you can proceed. Never forget that a flat battery is more likely to be a symptom of the trouble than the cause; there is almost certainly a short-circuit somewhere which has caused the battery to drain itself. It is possible for this to be a short-circuit inside the battery itself, so get the garage to check its condition at the same time as it is re-charged.

Once you are certain that the battery is all right you must check each individual lead in the circuit in question, a job made considerably easier by the fact that modern wiring harnesses use wires of distinctive colours for each of the individual circuits.

So, in the case of the specimen circuit to the tail lamp, you would, having checked first the bulb and then the battery, have disconnected the battery leads temporarily while the lighting switch was opened up. The end of the lead would then be freed from its terminal, brought clear, and the battery reconnected. The test rig would then have been applied to the open end of the lead; the holder placed against the lead and the holder wire connected to earth. If the lamp then lit it would show that current was reaching the terminal. Again disconnecting the battery, you would replace the lead you had removed and detach the end of the tail-lamp lead from the switch, connecting the test-rig lead in its place and earthing the holder. Then connect the battery and operate the switch. If it lights the bulb the switch has a clean bill of health, and the fault must lie either in the tail-lamp lead or in the lamp itself.

Continue checking, stage by stage, throughout the entire circuit. You may find, for example, that when the test rig is connected to the lamp end of the terminal it will not light the bulb. This shows that the fault lies in the lead itself. It has probably fractured, so it must be traced and inspected minutely. If it is a simple fracture you will find two loose ends. Sometimes a short-circuit can be detected by switching on and shaking the machine. As the broken end earths itself a characteristic crackling of electricity can be heard.

More difficult to locate is an internal fracture, where the insulation is undamaged. Garage men use a test rig fitted with a needle-sharp probe which can be pushed through the insulation at various points until a stage is reached at which the test bulb fails to light. This can, literally, pin-point the position of the breakage. An alternative is to pull two ways on the lead, at intervals of about three inches, until a section is found which stretches under such treatment. This is the section in which the break has occurred.

Where the suspect lead is a very long one, or is inaccessible, a double check and a temporary repair can be made by connecting the two terminals with an external length of wire. Sometimes, a new lead can be drawn through the conduit by wiring it to the old lead and pulling it through with it.

When repairing fractured leads it is important to ensure that no undue electrical stresses are set up and that the insulation is made good. All joints should be twisted together as neatly as possible—it is even better if they can be soldered—and the new joint must be wound round with insulating tape to make leakage impossible. Any terminals which have been undone must be refitted tightly, and if a soldered joint has failed it *must* be resoldered. It is not sufficient merely to tape it up.

Given patience and a modicum of equipment there is no reason why the average owner should not be able to trace most faults which can occur either in the engine or in the electrical system. Even when the nature of the failure is such that it is not possible to repair it oneself, it is often possible to provide a temporary cure, or at least to save money by giving the repairer an accurate diagnosis of the trouble.

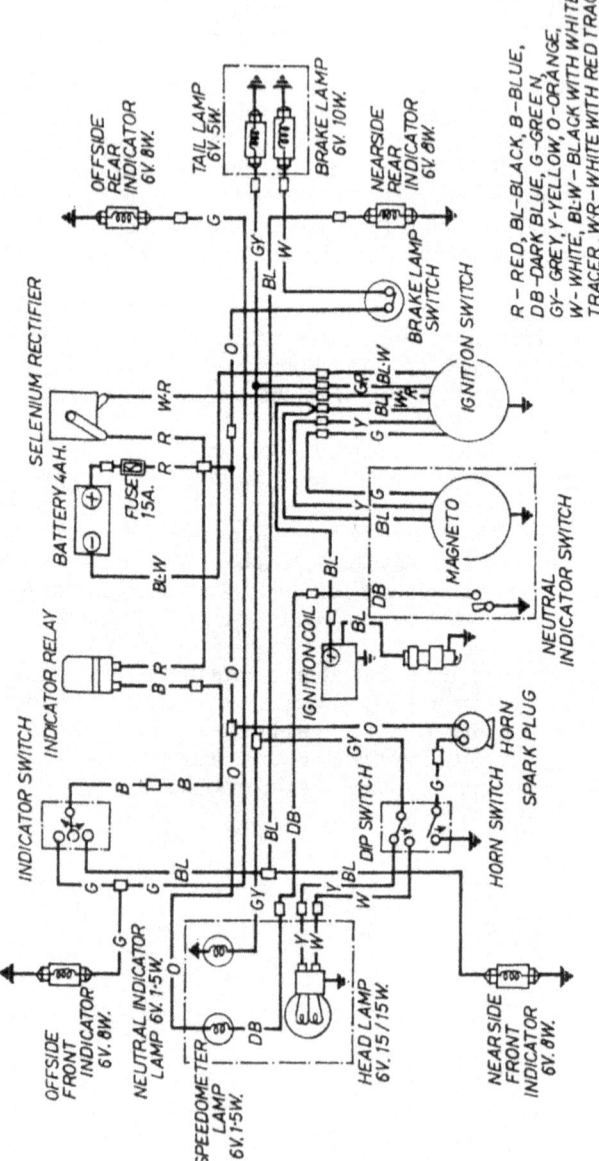

Fig. 56. Wiring Diagram, Model M 12 Sports

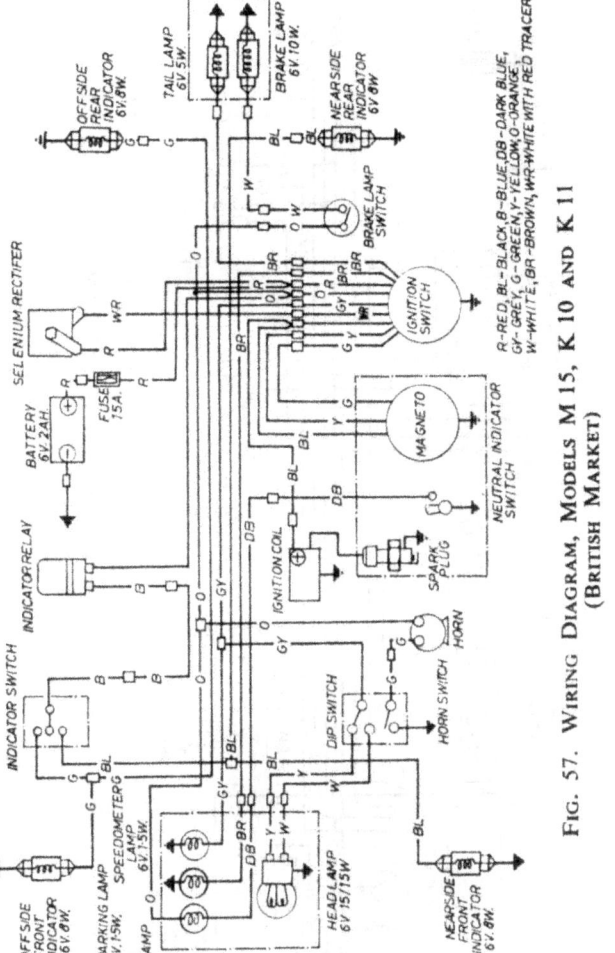

Fig. 57. Wiring Diagram, Models M 15, K 10 and K 11 (British Market)

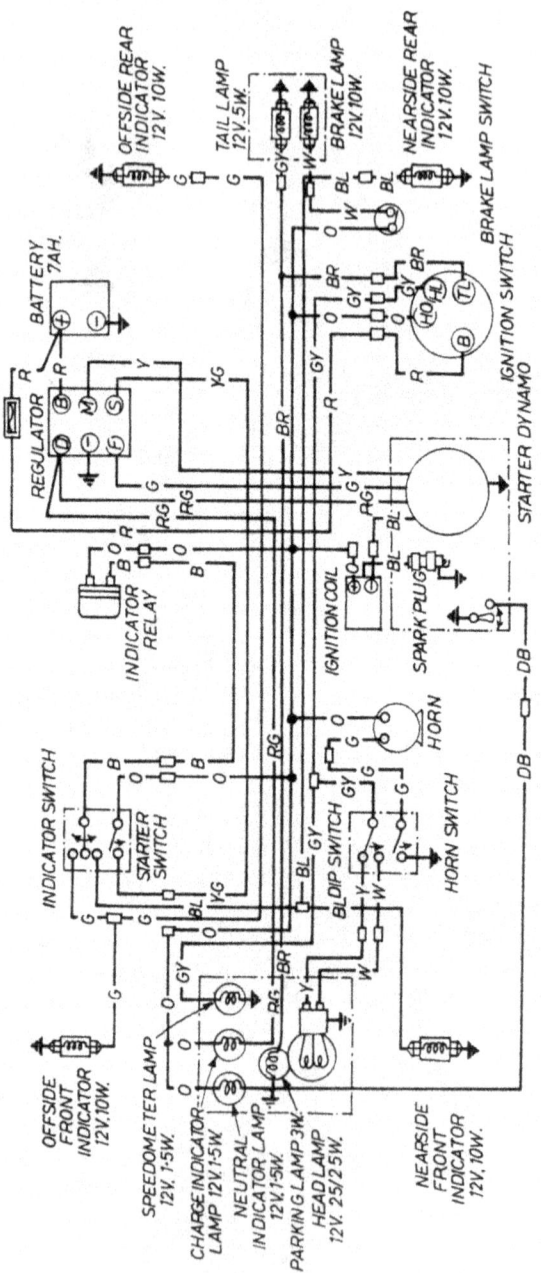

Fig. 58. Wiring Diagram, Model M 15 D, British Market

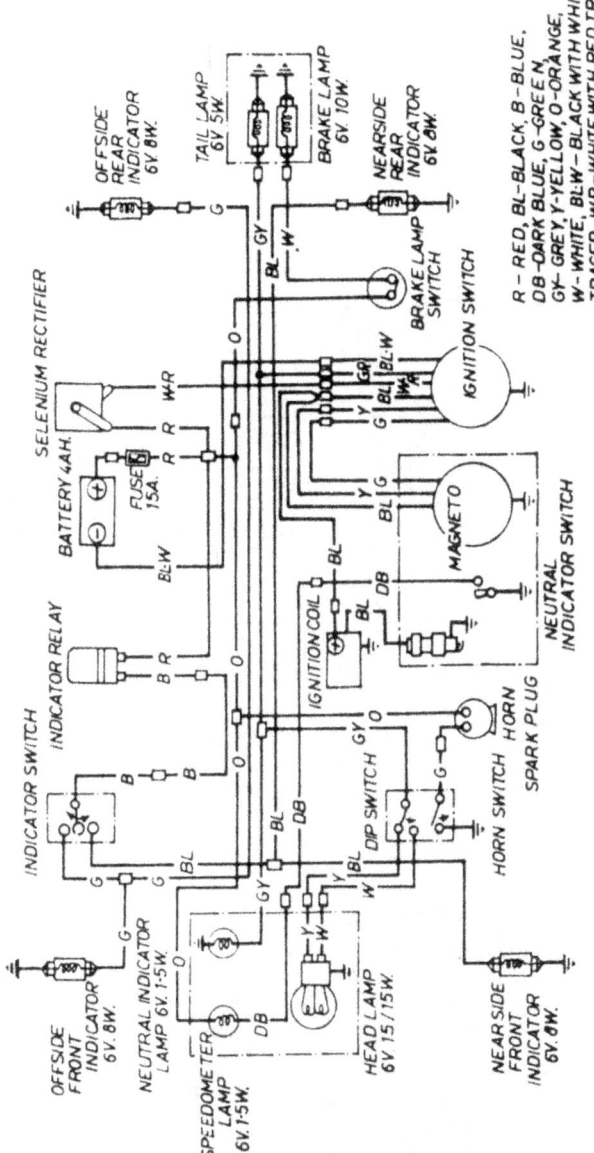

Fig. 59. Wiring Diagram, Models M 15, K 10 and K 11

This is the circuit used in markets other than Britain.

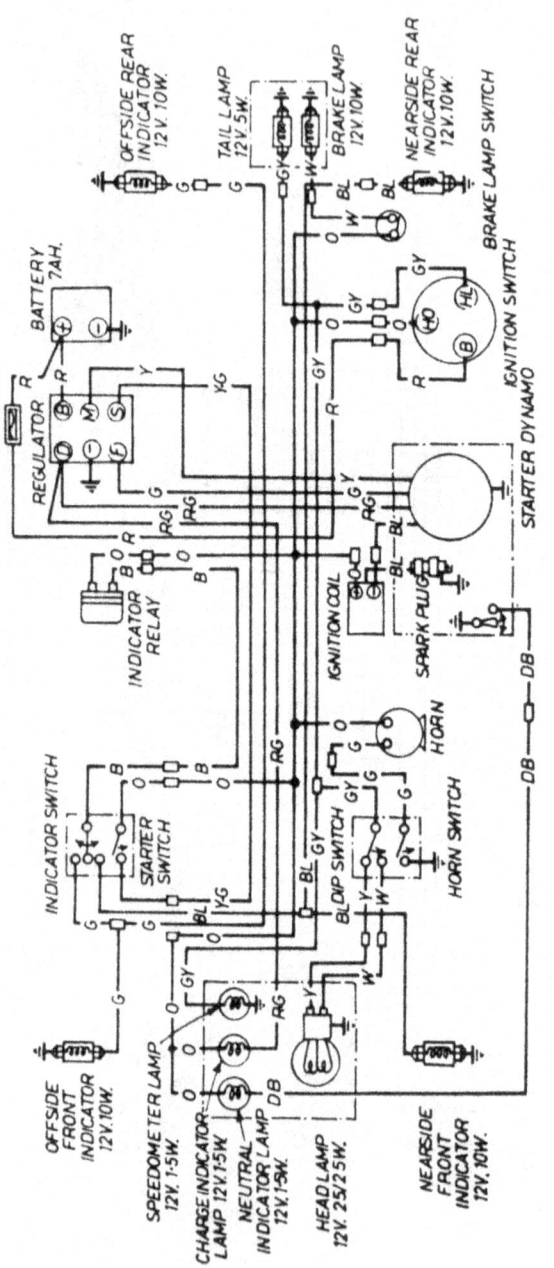

Fig. 60. Wiring Diagram, Model M 15 D
This is the circuit used in markets other than Britain.

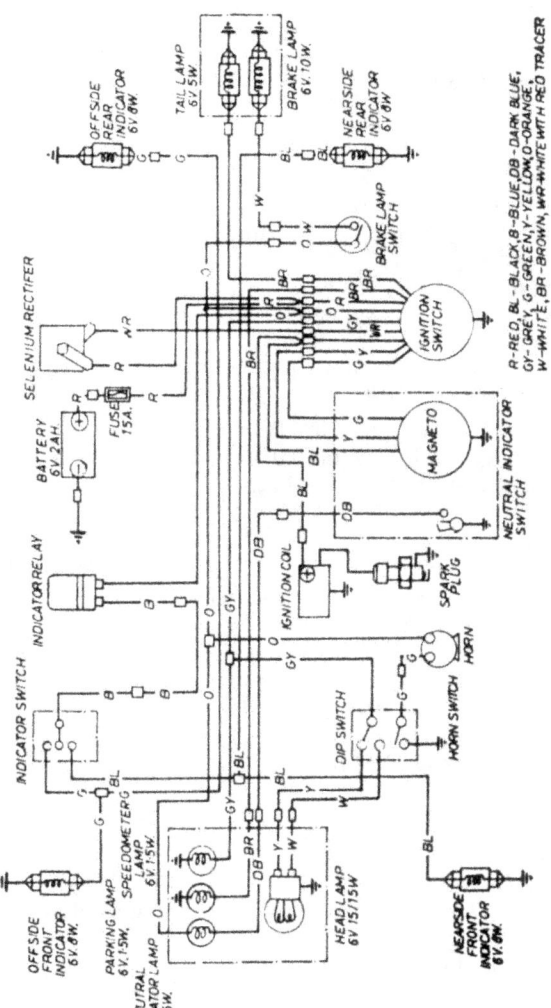

Fig. 61. Wiring Diagram, Model M 30 Suzy

# Appendix  Facts and Figures

## M 12, M 15 and M 15 D

*Bore:* 41 mm
*Stroke:* 38 mm
*Capacity:* 50 c.c.
*Compression ratio:* 7 : 1 (M 12 6·7 : 1)
*Recommended plugs:*  NGK B-6, Champion J-7 or J-6, Autolite A-5 Bosch W 175 T3
*Recommended fuel/oil ratio:* 20 : 1 (15 : 1 when running-in)
*Recommended lubricants:*  Shell 2T Two-stroke oil or equivalent. For gearbox, SAE 20/40 oil
*Tank capacity:* 1·32 gal (6 litres, 1·59 U.S. gal), inc. 1·8 pints reserve (1 litre, 2 U.S. pints)
*Sparking plug gap:* 0·5–0·7 mm (0·020–0·028 in.)
*Contact-breaker gap:* 0·3–0·4 mm (0·014–0·016 in.)
*Tyre size (front and rear):* 2·25 × 17 in.
*Tyre pressures:* 24 lb per sq in. (1·7 kg/sq cm) front; 30/32 lb per sq in. (2·1–2·3 kg/sq cm) rear
*Bulbs (M 12, M 15):* 6 V 15/15 W headlamp; 6 V 5 W tail lamp; 6 V 10 W stop lamp; 6 V 1·5 W speedometer light; 6 V 1·5 W neutral indicator; 6 V 8 W indicator lamps
*Bulbs (M 15 D):* 12 V 25/25 W headlamps; 12 V 5 W tail lamp; 12 V 10 W stop lamp; 12 V 1·5 W speedometer light; 12 V 1·5 W neutral indicator; 12 V 10 W direction indicators.
*Battery:* 6 V 4 amp-hr (M 12, M 15); 12 V 7 amp-hr (M 15 D)
*Fuse:* 15 amp (M 12 and M 15)

## M 30 Suzy

As above, except for—
*Compression ratio:* 6·3 : 1
*Tank capacity:* 0·77 gal (3·5 litres, 0·93 U.S. gal) inc. 0·9 pints (0·5 litres, 1 U.S. pint) reserve
*Battery:* 6 V 2 amp-hr

## K 10 and K 11

*Bore:* 45 mm
*Stroke:* 50 mm
*Capacity:* 79 c.c.
*Compression ratio:* 6·7 : 1

*Recommended plugs:* NGK B-6, Champion J-7 or J-6, Autolite A-5, Bosch W 175 T3

*Recommended fuel/oil ratio:* 20 : 1 (15 : 1 when running-in)

*Recommended lubricants:* Shell 2T Two-stroke oil or equivalent. For gearbox, SAE 20/40 oil. For front forks, 100 c.c. SAE 30 motor oil and 25 c.c. SAE 60 gear oil mixed

*Tank capacity:* 1·54 gal (7 litres, 1·85 U.S. gal), including 0·22 gal (1 litre, 0·26 U.S. gal) reserve

*Sparking plug gap:* 0·5–0·6 mm (0·020–0·024 in.)

*Contact-breaker gap:* 0·3–0·4 mm (0·012–0·016 in.)

*Tyre size (front and rear):* 2·50 × 17 in.

*Tyre pressures:* 20–26 lb per sq in. front; 29–40 lb per sq in. rear; according to load

*Bulbs:* 6 V 15/15 W headlamp; 6 V 5 W tail lamp; 6 V 10 W stop lamp; 6 V 1·5 W speedometer light; 6 V 1·5 W neutral indicator; 6 V 8 W direction indicators

*Battery:* 6 V 4 amp-hr

*Fuse:* 15 amp

### TYPICAL MAINTENANCE ROUTINE

*After 300 miles:* Clean and gap sparking plug; change transmission oil; adjust throttle cable to give 0·02–0·04 in. play; adjust idling speed; check contact-breaker setting and ignition timing and adjust if required; lightly oil the felt wick on contact-breaker cam; retighten cylinder head nuts; check battery specific gravity; clean petrol filter; adjust clutch cable to give 0·16-in. play at base of lever; lubricate drive chain and adjust to give 0·8–1·2-in. play with machine on stand; adjust brakes to give 0·8-in. play on each control; test all nuts, bolts and spokes.

*Every 2,000 miles:* As for the 300-mile service, plus—clean the air filter element; grease all nipples and lubricate cables.

*Every 4,000 miles:* As for the 2,000-mile service, plus—strip and clean the carburettor; decarbonize the cylinder head, piston crown, exhaust port, exhaust pipe and tail pipe; remove, wash and lubricate the drive chain; grease the brake operating cams.

# Index

AIR filter, cleaning, 30, 31
  purpose, 9
  removal, 30
  Suzy M 30, 24

BATTERY, construction, 39
  corrosion, 37
  removal, 45
  specific gravity, 38
  terminals, 37
  topping up, 37
  troubles, 38, 39
Brakes, construction, 15
  front, 70
  rear, 71
  shoes, 72

CARBURETTOR, cleaning, 28
  cutaway, 8, 30
  float chamber, 7, 8, 24
    removal, 25
  fuel filter, 9
    level, 27, 28
  gaskets, 28
  idling, setting, 28, 29
  jets, cleaning, 28
    general, 7, 8
    renewing, 27
  layout, 5, 6, 7, 8
  main jet, 8, 22
    removal, 25
  mixture, adjustment, 29, 30
  M 15/M 15D, removal, 42, 43
  needle jet, 8, 22
    removal, 25
    valve removal, 26, 27
  pilot jet, 8, 22
    removal, 26, 27
  starter, 8, 9, 23
    removal, 24, 27
  Suzy, removal of, 24, 44
  throttle, 7, 8, 22
    needle, 28
    slide, 24, 27, 28
Chain, links, 69
  M 15, removal of, 45
  M 30, removal of, 52

Circuit, faults, 75, 76, 77
  tester, 76
Clutch, construction, 14
  drawings, 58, 60, 61
  K 10/K 11, dismantling, 59, 61
  M 15/M 15D, dismantling, 48, 49
  M 30, dismantling, 54, 56
Contact-breaker, cleaning, 33, 34, 75
  gapping, 33
  points, 32, 33, 34, 75
  removal, 32
  stripping, 32

DECARBONIZING, exhaust system, 22
  methods, 21, 22
  ring grooves, 22

ENGINE, construction, 2
  cross-section, 1
  cycles, 2, 3, 4, 5
Engine, K 10/K 11
  barrel removal, 59
  carburettor removal, 57
  clutch cover removal, 59
    spring removal, 61
    stripping, 59
  gear selector removal, 62
  head removal, 57
  kickstarter spring removal, 62
  magneto removal, 59
  neutral indicator removal, 62
  removal complete, 57
  splitting crankcase, 62
  sprocket removal, 59
Engine, M 15/M 15D unit—
  barrel removal, 47
  bearings, insertion, 50
    removal, 50
  bolts, removal, 46
  carburettor clamp, 43
    controls, 43
  cleaning, 41
  crankcase, splitting, 49
  crankshaft, removal, 50
  cylinder bore wear, 47
  draining oil, 44
  drive sprocket removal, 48

# INDEX

Engine (contd.)—
  electrical leads, 42
  exhaust-pipe removal, 45
  flywheel removal, 47
  gear pedal removal, 44
    selector removal, 49
  head, removal, 46
  head nuts, tightening, 46
  kickstarter, removal, 45
    spring, removal, 48
  neutral indicator, removal, 48
  piston, removal, 50, 51
    rings, detaching, 50, 51
  primary drive, disconnecting, 49
  reassembly, general, 51
  removal, complete, 41
  rotor, detaching, 47
  stator plate, detaching, 47
  work *in situ*, 41, 42
Engine, M 30 Suzy unit—
  barrel, removal, 53
  clutch, assembly, 56
    removal, 54
  covers, removal, 54
  crankcase, splitting, 55
  flywheel, removal, 54
  gearchange, removal, 55
  head, removal, 53
  kickstarter, detaching, 54
  neutral indicator, removal, 54
  oil changing, 56
  piston, removal, 55
    rings, detaching, 55
  primary pinion, removing, 55
  rebuilding, complete, 55
  removal, complete, 52, 53
  sprocket, detaching, 54
  stator plate, removal, 54
  timing, ignition, 34, 35, 56

FLOODING, engine, clearing, 73, 74
Forks, front, removal, 65
  replacing, 66
  spring units, 66, 67
Fuel, petroil, 4, 5
  tap, cross-section, 31
  gasket, 31
  sludge trap, 31

GEARBOX, purpose, 13
  shafts, 13, 14

IGNITION, circuits, 10
  condenser, 13
  contact-breaker, 12, 32, 33, 34, 75
  generator, 10, 37
  layout, 9, 10
  magneto, 11
  sparking plug, 11, 13
  tests, 37
Ignition timing, flywheel models, 34, 35
  starter models, 35
  without dismantling, 35

K 10/K 11, bulbs and fuse, 85
  contact-breaker gap, 85
  dimensions, etc., 84, 85
  lubrication, 85
  recommended plugs, 85
  tyre pressures, 85

LIGHTING system, battery, 38, 39
  bulbs, 39, 85
  headlamp adjustment, 39
  lubricating switches, 39, 40
  wiring, 78, 79, 80, 81, 82, 83

M 12, M 15, M 15D, M 30, bulbs and fuses, 84
  contact-breaker gap, 84
  dimensions, etc., 84
  lubrication, 84
  recommended plugs, 84
  tyre pressures, 84

PRE-IGNITION, 75

REAR hub, exploded view, 69
Rear sprocket, replacement, 72
Routine maintenance, general, 85
  importance of, 19
  lubrication, 21
  recommended, 85
  task systems, 20, 21

SEIZURE, 75
Sparking plug, cap, 36
  cleaning, 35, 36
  "cold," 36
  drying, 74
  gapping, 36
  "hot," 36
  refitting, 36
  suppressor, 36

Sparking plug (*contd.*)—
  washer, 36
  "whiskered," 74
Steering, rake, 15
  theory, 15
  trail, 15
Steering head, adjustment, 63, 64
  bearings, 63
  bearing renewal, 64, 65, 66
Suspension, dampers, 15
  swinging link, 15
  telescopic, 15

TOOLS—
  adjustable spanners, 18
  box spanners, 16, 17
  feeler gauges, 33
  open-ended spanners, 16, 17
  pliers, 16, 17, 18
  points files, 33

Tools (*contd.*)—
  ring spanners, 16, 17
  scrapers, 22
  screwdrivers, 16, 18
  socket spanners, 16, 17
  special tools, 16, 47, 48, 49, 54, 55, 57, 59, 63, 68
  wire brushes, 22

WHEELS, bearing renewal, 71
  removal, 68, 69
  replacement, 71
Wiring diagrams—
  K 10/K 11 (British type), 79
  K 10/K 11 (foreign), 81
  M 12, 78
  M 15 (British type), 79
  M 15 (foreign), 81
  M 15D (British type), 80
  M 15D (foreign), 82
  M 30, 83

# OTHER CLASSIC MOTORCYCLE MANUALS CURRENTLY AVAILABLE IN THIS SERIES:

## AJS (BOOK OF) ALL MODELS 1955-1965:
350cc & 500cc Singles ~ Models 16,16S,18, 18S

## ARIEL WORKSHOP MANUAL 1933-1951:
All single, twin & 4 cylinder models

## ARIEL (BOOK OF) MAINTENANCE & REPAIR MANUAL 1932-1939:
LF3, LF4, LG, NF3, NF4, NG, OG, VA, VA3, VA4, VB, VF3, VF4, VG, Red Hunter LH, NH, OH, VH & Square Four 4F, 4G, 4H

## BMW FACTORY WORKSHOP MANUAL R27, R28:
English, German, French and Spanish text

## BMW FACTORY WORKSHOP MANUAL R50, R50S, R60, R69S:
Also includes a supplement for the USA models: R50US, R60US, R69US. English, German, French and Spanish text

## BSA PRE-WAR SINGLES & TWINS (BOOK OF) 1936-1939:
All Pre-War single & twin cylinder SV & OHV models through 1939
150cc, 250cc, 350cc, 500cc, 600cc, 750cc & 1,000cc

## BSA SINGLES (BOOK OF) 1945-1954:
OHV & SV 250cc, 350cc, 500cc & 600cc, Groups B, C & M

## BSA SINGLES (BOOK OF) 1955-1967:
B31, B32, B33, B34 and "Star" B40 & SS90

## BSA 250cc SINGLES (BOOK OF) 1954-1970:
B31, B32, B33, B34 and "Star" B40 & SS90

## BSA TWINS (BOOK OF) 1948-1962:
All 650cc & 500cc twins

## BSA TWINS (SECOND BOOK OF) 1962-1969:
All 650cc & 500cc, A50 & A65 OHV unit construction twins

## DUCATI OHC FACTORY WORKSHOP MANUAL:
160 Junior Monza, 250 Monza, 250 GT, 250 Mark 3, 250 Mach 1, 250 SCR & 350 Sebring

## HONDA 250 & 305cc FACTORY WORKSHOP MANUAL:
C.72 C.77 CS.72, CS.77, CB.72, CB.77 [HAWK]

## HONDA 125 & 150cc FACTORY WORKSHOP MANUAL:
C.92, CS.92, CB.92, C.95 & CA.95

## HONDA 90 (BOOK OF) ALL MODELS UP TO 1966:
All 90cc variations including the S90, CM90, C200, S65, Trail 90 & C65 models

**HONDA 50cc FACTORY WORKSHOP MANUAL:** C.100

**HONDA 50cc FACTORY WORKSHOP MANUAL:** C.110

**HONDA (BOOK OF) MAINTENANCE & REPAIR 1960-1966:**
50cc C.100, C.102, C.110 & C.114 ~ 125cc C.92 & CB.92
250cc C.72 & CB.72 ~ 305cc CB.77

**LAMBRETTA (BOOK OF) MAINTENANCE & REPAIR:**
125 & 150cc, all models up to 1958, except model "48".

**LAMBRETTA (SECOND BOOK OF) MAINTENANCE & REPAIR:**
125, 150, 175 & 200cc, all Li & TV models and derivates from 1958 to 1970.

**NORTON FACTORY TWIN CYLINDER WORKSHOP MANUAL 1957-1970:** *Lightweight Twins:* 250cc Jubilee, 350cc Navigator and 400cc Electra and the *Heavyweight Twins:* Model 77, 88, 88SS, 99, 99SS, Sports Special, Manxman, Mercury, Atlas, G15, P11, N15, Ranger (P11A).

**NORTON (BOOK OF) MAINTENANCE & REPAIR 1932-1939:**
All Pre-War SV, OHV and OHC models: 16H, 16I, 18, 19, 20, 50, 55, ES2, CJ, CSI, International 30 & 40

**SUZUKI 200 & 250cc FACTORY WORKSHOP MANUAL:**
250cc T20 [X-6 Hustler] ~ 200cc T200 [X-5 Invader & Sting Ray Scrambler]

**SUZUKI 250cc FACTORY WORKSHOP MANUAL:** 250cc ~ T10

**TRIUMPH (BOOK OF) MAINTENANCE & REPAIR 1935-1939:**
All Pre-War single & twin cylinder models: L2/1, 2/1, 2/5, 3/1, 3/2, 3/5, 5/1, 5/2, 5/3, 5/4, 5/5, 5/10, 6/1, Tiger 70, 80, 90 & 2H. Tiger 70C, 3S & 3H, Tiger 80C & 5H, Tiger 90C, 6S, 2HC & 3SC, 5T & 5S and T100

**TRIUMPH 1937-1951 WORKSHOP MANUAL (A. St. J. Masters):**
Covers rigid frame and sprung hub single cylinder SV & OHV and twin cylinder OHV pre-war, military, and post-war models

**TRIUMPH 1945-1955 FACTORY WORKSHOP MANUAL NO.11:**
Covers pre-unit, twin-cylinder rigid frame, sprung hub, swing-arm and 350cc, 500cc & 650cc.

**VELOCETTE (BOOK OF) MAINTENANCE & REPAIR:**
Covers LE Mk. I, II, & III, Valiant, Vogue, MOV, MAC, KSS, KTS, Viper, Venom & Thruxton. Includes some limited material on the Viceory scooter

**VESPA (BOOK OF) MAINTENANCE & REPAIR 1946-1959:**
All 125cc & 150cc models including 42/L2 & Gran Sport

**VINCENT WORKSHOP MANUAL 1935-1955:**
All Series A, B & C Models

~ WWW.VELOCEPRESS.COM ~

www.ingramcontent.com/pod-product-compliance
Lightning Source LLC
Chambersburg PA
CBHW070601170426
43201CB00012B/1899